MW00652949

SINGLE CASE RESEARCH
IN SCHOOLS

Single Case Research in Schools addresses and examines the variety of cutting-edge issues in single case research (SCR) in educational settings. Featuring simple and practical techniques for aggregating data for evidence-based practices, the book delves into methods of selecting behaviors of interest and measuring them reliably.

The latter part of *Single Case Research in Schools* is devoted to a step-by-step model of using SCR to evaluate practices in schools. This includes considerations such as measurement, data collection, length of phases, design considerations, calculating effect size, and reliability of measures.

Kimberly J. Vannest, PhD, is an associate professor in the department of educational psychology at Texas A & M University. She has published more than eighty books, peer-reviewed publications, and software on the topic of intervention, progress monitoring, and single design. She has received awards for her research, teaching, and service and speaks internationally on the topic of single case research.

John L. Davis, MA, LSSP, is a doctoral candidate in the department of educational psychology at Texas A & M University. He is a licensed specialist in school psychology with over ten years experience of providing direct service in schools. He has published on topics including measurement considerations in response to intervention, acceptability of intervention protocols in schools, and assessment of students with emotional disturbance and autism.

Richard I. Parker, PhD, is professor emeritus at Texas A & M University. He has published more than one hundred articles on this and related topics, and continues his scholarship in single case research and design. He currently lives in California.

School-Based Practice in Action Series
Series Editors
Rosemary B. Mennuti, EdD, NCSP
and
Ray W. Christner, PsyD, NCSP
Cognitive Health Solutions, LLC

This series provides school-based practitioners with concise practical guidebooks that are designed to facilitate the implementation of evidence-based programs into school settings, putting the best practices *in action*.

Assessment and Intervention for Executive Function Difficulties
George McCloskey, Lisa A. Perkins, and Bob Van Divner

Resilient Playgrounds
Beth Doll

Comprehensive Planning for Safe Learning Environments: A School Counselor's Guide to Integrating Physical and Psychological Safety – Prevention through Recovery
Melissa A. Reeves, Linda M. Kanan, Amy E. Plog

Behavioral Interventions in Schools: A Response-to-Intervention Guidebook
David M. Hulac, Joy Terrell, Odell Vining, and Joshua Bernstein

The Power of Family-School Partnering (FSP): A Practical Guide for School Mental Health Professionals and Educators
Cathy Lines, Gloria Miller, and Amanda Arthur-Stanley

Implementing Response-to-Intervention in Elementary and Secondary Schools: Procedures to Assure Scientific-Based Practices, Second Edition
Matthew K. Burns and Kimberly Gibbons

A Guide to Psychiatric Services in Schools: Understanding Roles, Treatment, and Collaboration
Shawna S. Brent

Comprehensive Children's Mental Health Services in Schools and Communities
Robyn S. Hess, Rick Jay Short, and Cynthia Hazel

Responsive School Practices to Support Lesbian, Gay, Bisexual, Transgender, and Questioning Students and Families
Emily Fisher and Kelly Kennedy

Pediatric School Psychology: Conceptualization, Applications, and Leadership Development
Thomas J. Power and Kathy L. Bradley-Klug

Serving the Gifted: Evidence-Based Clinical and Psychoeducational Practice
Steven I. Pfeiffer

Early Childhood Education: A Practical Guide to Evidence-Based, Multi-Tiered Service Delivery
Gina Coffee, Corey E. Ray-Subramanian, G. Thomas Schanding, Jr., and Kelly A. Feeney-Kettler

Implementing Response-to-Intervention to Address the Needs of English-Language Learners: Instructional Strategies and Assessment Tools for School Psychologists
Holly Hudspath-Niemi and Mary Lou Conroy

Conducting Student-Driven Interviews: Practical Strategies for Increasing Student Involvement and Addressing Behavior Problems
John Murphy

Single Case Research in Schools: Practical Guidelines for School-Based Professionals
Kimberly J. Vannest, John L. Davis, and Richard I. Parker

SINGLE CASE RESEARCH IN SCHOOLS

Practical Guidelines for School-Based Professionals

Kimberly J. Vannest,
John L. Davis, and
Richard I. Parker

Routledge
Taylor & Francis Group

NEW YORK AND LONDON

First published 2013
by Routledge
711 Third Avenue, New York, NY 10017

Simultaneously published in the UK
by Routledge
27 Church Road, Hove, East Sussex BN3 2FA

© 2013 Taylor & Francis

Routledge is an imprint of the Taylor & Francis Group, an informa business

The right of Kimberly J. Vannest, John L. Davis & Richard I. Parker to be
identified as authors of this work has been asserted by them in accordance with
sections 77 and 78 of the Copyright, Designs and Patents Act 1988.

All rights reserved. No part of this book may be reprinted or reproduced or
utilised in any form or by any electronic, mechanical, or other means, now
known or hereafter invented, including photocopying and recording, or in any
information storage or retrieval system, without permission in writing from the
publishers.

Trademark notice: Product or corporate names may be trademarks or registered
trademarks, and are used only for identification and explanation without intent
to infringe.

Library of Congress Cataloging in Publication Data
Vannest, Kimberly J., 1967–
    Single case research in schools : practical guidelines for school-based
    professionals / Kimberly J. Vannest, John L. Davis & Richard I. Parker.
        pages cm — (School based practice in action series)
    Includes bibliographical references and index.
    1. Education—Research—Methodology.   2. Single subject research.
    I. Davis, John L. (Lockett), 1977–   II. Parker, Richard I.   III. Title.
    LB1028.S5118 2013
    370.72—dc23   2012047193

ISBN: 978–0–415–64166–1 (hbk)
ISBN: 978–0–415–64167–8 (pbk)
ISBN: 978–0–203–08142–6 (ebk)

Typeset in Baskerville
by Swales & Willis Ltd, Exeter, Devon

SUSTAINABLE
FORESTRY
INITIATIVE

Certified Sourcing
www.sfiprogram.org
SFI-00555
The SFI label applies to the text stock.

Printed and bound in the United States of America by
Walsworth Publishing Company, Marceline, MO.

DEDICATION

Kimberly Vannest would like to dedicate this book to Jack and Randy, Frank and Karen. Thank you for love and support these many long days and late nights. I could not have done this without you. Also my heartfelt gratitude to Rich and Yupadee Parker, mentors and friends. My life would not be nearly as rich as it is today without your many gifts of wisdom and your endless patience: "khob-kun-Ka"—Thank you.

John Davis would like to dedicate this book to his loving and supportive wife Heather.

CONTENTS

SERIES EDITORS' FOREWORD

We are delighted to see the continued growth of the School-Based Practice in Action series, which grew out of a discussion between us several years ago while attending a professional conference. At that time, we were each at different points in our careers, yet we both realized and faced the same challenges for education and serving children and families. Acknowledging the transformations facing the educational system, we shared a passion and vision in ensuring quality services to schools, students, and families. This vision involved increasing the strong knowledge base of practitioners together with an impact on service delivery. This would require the need to understand theory and research, albeit we viewed the most critical element as having the needed resources bridging empirical knowledge to the process of practice. Thus, our goal for the School-Based Practice in Action series has been to offer resources for readers based on sound research and principles that can be set directly "into action."

To accomplish this, each book in the series offers information in a practice-friendly manner. The books are designed to have a direct impact on transitioning research and knowledge into the day-to-day functions of school-based practitioners. We recognize that the implementation of programs and the changing of roles come with challenges and barriers, and as such, these may take on various forms depending on the context of the situation and the voice of the practitioner. To that end, the books of the School-Based Practice in Action series may be used in their entirety and present form for a number of practitioners; however, for others, these books will help them find new ways to move toward effective action and new possibilities. No matter which style fits your practice, we hope that these books will influence your work and professional growth.

It has been a pleasure having the opportunity to work with Drs Kimberly J. Vannest, John L. Davis, and Richard I. Parker in the development of this book, *Single Case Research in Schools: Practical Guidelines for School-Based Professionals*. Given the increased need for data-based decision-making and evidence-based practice within educational settings, we felt it was necessary to have a book in the series that could offer practice-friendly guidelines for school-based providers on using single-case design research in their practice. Vannest, Davis, and Parker exceeded our expectations in delivering this book. *Single Case Research in Schools* takes concepts that many practitioners find overwhelming and describes them in terms that are both user-friendly and directly related to evaluating services in schools. The authors make direct suggestions on how to use single-case design to evaluate services, monitor progress, and make decisions, and there is specific attention given to ensuring the reliability of the data used. Although it is not easy to make a book on research "come alive," Vannest, Davis, and Parker were able to do so through the numerous case examples provided, which will enable readers to use the information in this book and take direct actions within their work environments. We are pleased to have *Single Case Research in Schools* as part of our book series.

Finally, we want to extend our gratitude to Ms. Anna Moore and Routledge for their ongoing support of a book series focused on enriching the practice and service delivery within school settings. Their openness to meet the needs of school-based practitioners made the *School-Based Practice in Action* series possible. In addition, we must thank Mr. Dana Bliss, whose interest and collaboration made our idea for a book series a reality. We hope that you enjoy reading and implementing the materials in this book and the rest of the series as much as we have enjoyed working with the authors on developing these resources. Best wishes in your work with schools, children, and families.

Rosemary B. Mennuti, EdD, NCSP
Ray W. Christner, PsyD, NCSP
Series Editors, School-Based Practice in Action Series

ACKNOWLEDGEMENTS

The authors acknowledge the support and assistance of friends and family who went to great lengths to make time available for the writing of this book. Also to our editors for their patience with our work and thoughtful review of the material. To our students who assisted in all manner of data collection, reference gathering, and discussions about the material contained within. Finally, to the professionals in schools whose work informs ours on a routine basis.

John Davis would also like to acknowledge his co-authors and mentors Dr. Vannest and Dr. Parker for introducing him to the study of single case research and inspiring his work on this topic.

1

HISTORY AND SIGNIFICANCE
OF SINGLE CASE RESEARCH

This chapter overviews the components that make single case research unique and provides a brief background regarding the origins of SCR and its application in schools. The aim of this chapter is to provide a basic introduction for readers with little to no background and to set up the context for what follows in subsequent chapters.

What is Single Case Research?

Single case research (SCR) is the study of the individual. This could be one individual or many individuals, but at its heart, the unit of analysis is "one" person. This individual serves as a "control" against him- or herself. SCR is an extremely important tool in schools and clinical settings because the problems faced by children and individuals with disabilities are often unique. Sara, for example, is a second grade girl with selective mutism at school, a high IQ, and problem behaviors in the cafeteria and school library that include hiding under tables and desks and pinching children who walk by. Sara's behavior has not responded to teacher reprimands, parents being called to take her home or timeouts in library and cafeteria spaces. Michael meanwhile is a ninth grade boy with Prader-Willi syndrome and an unassessed IQ who eats the laminate off the edge of the school desks but performs reasonably well in classes. Michael's odd behaviors evoke classroom disruptions when other students make comments or tease. Michael's preferred responses to comments of his peers or teacher include pulling his pants down or leaving the classroom, neither of which are workable in the setting.

SCR's usefulness comes in part from its multi-purpose nature. SCR can involve a comparison between a treatment condition and a non-treatment condition, for example Condition 1 or phase A—length of time getting dressed independently—and Condition 2 or phase B—length of time getting dressed independently with music playing. SCR can also involve more than one treatment condition, for example accuracy of homework completion with a peer tutor, accuracy of homework completion with a peer tutor and reinforcement for scores above 90 percent, and accuracy of homework completion with no peer tutor and scores above 90 percent.

The designs of SCR are purposeful in order to control for threats to validity in a study (more on this topic in Chapter 2). The data in SCR is described as time series data, meaning that measurements are repeated across time. The stock market and the weather are common examples of time series data.

In addition to an individual subject of interest, a purposeful design, and time series data, SCR requires a well-defined target or targets (for example, getting dressed or homework completion and accuracy), consistent measurement (for example, length of time), and equivalence of measures and environmental conditions (see Figure 1.1).

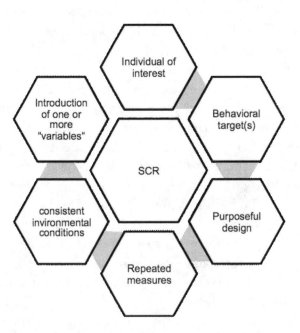

Figure 1.1 **Single case research (SCR) has specific requirements.**

Within an SCR design one condition serves as a control for the other condition. For example, Sara's behavior under typical conditions could be represented by operationally defining and counting the frequency of these problem episodes, and her word use could also be counted. This is considered a baseline condition. Michael's baseline would also be an empirical representation of his behaviors and might include inappropriate responses to comments from peers, or his pica behavior (eating inedible items) (see Figure 1.2).

SCR designs compare performances in conditions that are adjacent. A to B or B to C. Baseline phase sets the condition of "current

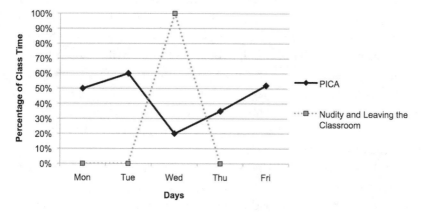

Figure 1.2 **Baseline data for Sara and Michael.**

performance" or the control condition of what behavior looks like prior to treatment or intervention. Baseline or phase A is also represented by nomenclature such as A1 or A_1 and these terms are interchangeable, although some professionals will have preferences and justifications for one over another.

The data represented in Figures 1.1 and 1.2 is only as good as the measures used to collect it. The measures used in SCR can include direct observation, self-report in the form of questionnaires or surveys, or inferential sources such as rating forms or retrospective remembrances. The data can be anything from a frequency count to a topographical description including scales of any number, rates or percentage. For example, Sara's frequency of pinching could also be represented by a scale score 1–10 about the amount of social interaction with peers. Michael's data could be a self-assessment about his time on task (as a replacement for pica) or an A–F category scale for the nudity and elopement: "A" would be no departure or nudity and "F" would be pants off and walking out the door; "C" might be starting to leave the room with pants up but returning when asked, etc. The data (in any form) must be reliable. More on the topic of reliability will be discussed later in Chapter 5.

Single case research is a broadly used research methodology commonly seen in psychology, education, and increasingly in medicine. It is particularly well suited for closely examining the effect of X on Y. In fact, you may notice many published titles of studies will be variants of this, for example, "What is the effect of X on Y." SCR is frequently seen in psychology and education because the problems of concern tend to be very specific, sometimes unique, and may be related to a naturalistic setting. For example, Michael's Prader-Willi syndrome and associated behaviors such as eating the laminate off the corner of his desk in Language Arts class is a problem not easily solved or examined in "large n" studies (those with, say, 200 participants in a control group and 200 in a treatment group). In fact, it is this "applied" characteristic that makes SCR so appealing.

Single case research has been the bedrock of the educational sciences related to disability since the early 1960s, meaning that individual treatments have been applied with the goal of solving practical, socially important problems.

In the 1960s and 1970s researchers in applied sciences began to call for an alignment in methodology to evaluate the effects of intervention. As new theories and procedures started to emerge, researchers began to champion certain methods for measuring intervention effects (Paul, 1969). One of the primary methods in use during this time was the "case study" method of investigation (Bolger, 1965). This was a move away from group research (Bergin & Strupp, 1970; Estes, 1956) and many began to advocate the use of single case studies as a better way to describe certain phenomena and control for threats to validity (Bergin & Strupp, 1970; Dukes 1965; Shapiro, 1961).

SCR can tell us about causal relationships, for example, "Does the use of a daily behavior report card (DBRC) reduce office discipline referrals (ODRs)?" SCR can also tell us about the differences between treatment options, for example, "Does a DBRC or self-monitoring work better to reduce ODRs?", or even about multiple treatment options as in component analysis—"does a DBRC without reinforcement and a DBRC with reinforcement and a DBRC with reinforcement and check-in and check-out result in the most improved behavior?"

Thus SCR is useful for examining individuals and their problems, but SCR is also useful in defending evidence-based practices. SCR can provide a "rigorous experimental evaluation of intervention effects (Horner & Spaulding, in press; Kazdin, 1982; Kratochwill, 1978; Kratochwill & Levin, 1992; Shadish, Cook, & Campbell, 2002)" (Kratochwill et al., 2010, p. 2).

Multiple studies of SCR data can also be aggregated to provide measures of effects, confidence intervals, and insight into the moderators associated with efficacious use. This is particularly important for evidence-based practice determination and in making recommendations to the field about the adoption, sustainability, and fidelity of implementation of treatments.

A Very Brief History

Operant psychology set the foundation for what is now Applied Behavior Analysis (ABA), a branch of inquiry most responsible for promoting the use of SCR. Skinner, Lindsley, and others operated labs at Harvard University from 1956 to 1961, originating the term "behavior therapy." In 1961, when Lindsley moved to the University of Kansas his work began to propagate a new discipline in the training of special educators and researchers. Elsewhere in the early 1960s, Bijou and Baer at the University of Washington were engaged in pioneering work in ABA with students and adults with exceptional characteristics (Bijou & Baer, 1961). The methods for evaluating change and treatment effectiveness emerged from this work. Sidman's 1960 text, *Tactics of scientific research: evaluating experimental data in psychology*, represents the early thinking on SCR design and inter-pretation. General guidelines included an emphasis on the visual analysis of repeated, large, and convincing changes in behavior "that is, those large enough to be clear to anyone." More specific guidelines for visual judgments were lacking, but clearly observable (large) effects served as a quality indicator, ideally representing environmental con-trol, good measures, strong valid design, and as an indication of adequate attention to the threats to internal validity.

The two earliest journals to publish this operant behavioral research were the *Journal for the Experimental Analysis of Behavior* (*JEAB*) (1958), and a more applied offshoot, the *Journal of Applied Behavior Analysis* (*JABA*) (1968). The two journals distinguish two purposes of ABA. *JEAB* focused on scientific inquiry to establish functional relationships between interventions and behavioral change via a strong causal inference (Sidman, 1960; Skinner, 1966). *JABA* emphasized the application of operant principles to solve practical, socially important problems.

Questions Answered by Single Case Research

Historically, two primary purposes for single case research exist: basic research and applied research. These purposes involve different types of questions. Basic research is about the demonstration of a functional relationship. A functional relationship is defined as a relationship in which one variable changes systematically in relationship to the other. In order to demonstrate a functional relationship four conditions must be present (see Figures 1.3 and 1.4):

1. There must be a consistent response to stimulus change and only to stimulus change.

2. Replications must be enough to discount other potential causes of behavior change.
3. The change must be large enough to be visually convincing.
4. Patterns should be unambiguous and without anomalies.

In contrast to basic research, applied research is interested in whether or not there is/was enough change to "improve a client's life." These types of questions require all of the criteria involved in basic research *plus* the notion of socially valid target behaviors (by clients in need). The issue of clinical or practical significance comes into play here as well. Is the change large enough to make a practical difference in the quality of life? In applied research the following conditions must be present:

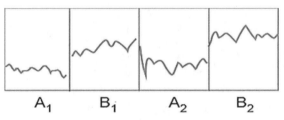

A_1 B_1 A_2 B_2

*Convincing Magnitude of Change +

*Sufficient Replications +

*Patterns Unambiguous (without Anomalies)

= Functional Relationship

Figure 1.3 **Hypothetical data demonstrating a functional relationship.**

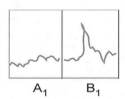

A_1 B_1

*Replications Too Few or
*Small Magnitude of Change or
*Ambiguous Data Pattern

= No Functional Relationship

Figure 1.4 **Hypothetical data and design demonstrating no functional relationship.**

1. There must be a consistent response to stimulus change and only to stimulus change.
2. Replications must be enough to discount other potential causes of behavior change.
3. The change must be large enough to be visually convincing.
4. Patterns should be unambiguous and without anomalies.
5. Target behaviors must be socially valid.
6. Change must be practically significant.

Single case research is incredibly useful for a variety of purposes. In applied settings SCR methods allow us to closely examine behavior change and determine the relevant features of the environment and how those interact with the characteristics of the individual. For example, Ruby throws small tantrums when it is time to get dressed in the morning or on the way to school. An SCR study sets up a mechanism to collect data, implement an intervention, and determine effects. SCR in this instance is well aligned with applied behavior analysis. We may take baseline data on the occurrence and length of Ruby's tantrums, hypothesize that her tantrums occur when she is watching cartoons, and devise an intervention that incorporates a routine of the TV off before and as a part of the transition toward breakfast (a more preferred activity). Getting dressed would then be after breakfast and no longer associated as the reason for no TV. If data collection during intervention demonstrated that Ruby was no longer tantruming, or that tantruming began to lessen, we might infer that the intervention of a schedule change was successful in changing Ruby's behavior (see Figure 1.5).

This is an example of what we might call a "low-stakes" decision. The consequences are rather small if an error is made in inferring change when none occurred. Furthermore, the ability to revisit a decision and change intervention to something greater or lesser is easily done at any point in time. This is also an example of an AB design, where A represents baseline and B represents the intervention.

What if Ruby's tantruming didn't change or didn't change enough, though? Let us suppose that Ruby tantrums less, but the pattern she picked up is now a habit and getting dressed to go to school may not

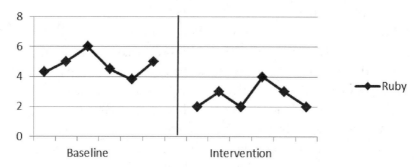

Figure 1.5 **Example of AB design.**

be appealing. So although the antecedent schedule change improved behavior some, the consequences have yet to be adjusted. If tantrum behavior still needs decreasing you could introduce a C phase (see Figure 1.6). Making this an ABC design. C phase might be activity, edible, or tangible reinforcement (sitting in the front seat on the way to school or juice or milk in the car for the ride, or earning stickers towards a stuffed animal) for getting dressed happily.

These designs (AB and ABC) are ideal for scenarios where a "little" information or documentation is needed about behavior change but

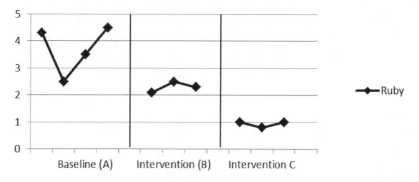

Figure 1.6 **Example ABC design.**

the reason for the change is less important. In other words, if Ruby's behavior actually changed because she was sleeping more at night or because of the attention paid as a result of monitoring the behavior it is probably less than critical.

Sometimes decisions, however, are not low-stake decisions. Some decisions have large consequences, are irrevocable, or are less frequently reviewed for change. So these decisions have greater impact, more staying power, and are less likely to be undone and thus more likely to cause damage if they are wrong. With high or higher-stakes decisions we need to accurately infer cause. Cause in single case research is equivalent to a functional relationship. When one event happens, the other event happens. When I turn on a light switch, the light comes on. When I compliment a friend, the friend smiles and says "thank you." Determining whether functional relationships exist is not an absolute certainty, but they are high-probability events. Later in the book we will discuss how to identify the relative certainty of behavior change.

To illustrate how SCR would determine a functional relationship let's introduce Scarlett. Scarlett is in a class of ten and during reading instruction she drops to her knees and pretends to be a cat. Scarlett's teacher frequently sends Scarlett out of the classroom and she misses critical reading instruction. As a replacement strategy for sending Scarlett out of class, an intervention is suggested for the teacher to ask Scarlett to be the one to call the class to reading and to ask Scarlett to read first. Because the teacher is resistant to this idea and believes Scarlett needs to be removed, an ABAB design is used to demonstrate the effect of Scarlett calling the class to reading and Scarlett reading first. Cat-like behavior is recorded as a simple "yes/no". Baseline data and intervention data (A1B1) show an immediate and sustained decrease in cat-like behavior when the intervention is introduced. Reintroducing the A condition (removal of intervention) demonstrates that the cat-like behavior is controlled by Scarlett calling the group to reading and then reading first because when this strategy is removed, the cat-like behavior returns. A reintroduction of the intervention results in a reversal of the behavior once again (see Figure 1.7). More demonstrations or replications provide more evidence of the effect (ABAB or ABABAB).

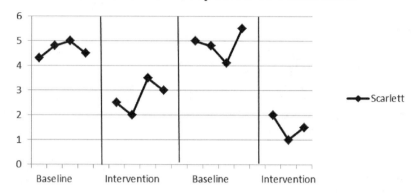

Figure 1.7 **Example of ABAB or reversal design.**

There are times, however, when behavior change will not reverse. Jack is a sixth-grader in seventh-grade math. When homework is assigned, Jack hides the homework in his backpack or locker and doesn't bring it home. When "caught" and asked why, he says he needs help understanding the assignments and can't do the work. The teacher introduces a new method for solving the problems and Jack learns the steps involved in pre-algebra. This "learning" cannot be reversed, and so the gains demonstrated in intervention are unlikely to reverse when the intervention is removed and "hiding homework" behavior is unlikely to reverse to previous states, because help was needed and help provided. In such an example neither an AB nor an ABAB design will be effective for telling us what we need to know. Here, we need a multiple baseline design.

A multiple baseline design (MBD) allows for "assurance" or "more certainty" about the effects of an intervention or treatment through replication. Replication of the effect of one event on another is created through the use of multiple people or multiple places or time. This is referred to as across settings, or across participants, or multiple baseline across settings, or multiple baseline across participants, or multiple baseline across behaviors.

Figure 1.8 shows a second student receiving the same intervention (individual instruction) at a later time. The staggered start to the intervention allows us a "replication" of the effect without expecting

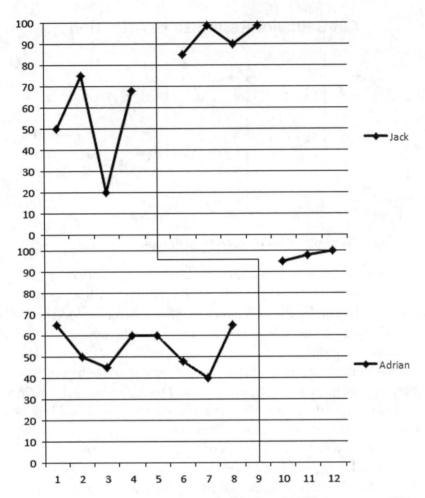

Figure 1.8 **Example multiple baseline design for algebra scores "The Effect of Individual Instruction on Homework Score."**

learning to reverse. Done enough times this replication could demonstrate a functional relationship between individual instruction and improved grades. Just as an ABAB demonstrated effects three times (A1 to B1, B1 to A2, A2 to B2), multiple baselines with three changes could demonstrate the same principle.

Conclusion Validity

Conclusion validity or internal validity is the degree to which the "results" can be trusted. Can you draw a "conclusion" from your own work? There are many "threats" to validity. Poor measures or poor reliability would make the results questionable. You would be unable to draw a sound conclusion. The two primary methods for addressing threats to internal validity are (a) "strong design," (b) solid measurement, and (c) "replication."

Strong design controls for alternative explanations to the behavior change. If I give Jack candy and Jack starts acting energetic, one might say, "Oh, he had sugar." Perhaps, however, he is just excited about candy. Perhaps candy is a part of a celebration, or maybe he didn't get enough rest and adrenaline kicked in. For any event there are many possible explanations for the behavior change, control helps eliminate those alternative explanations. One part of this control is to systematically manipulate or vary the independent variable (treatment or intervention). Another part of this control is systematic accurate measurement (reliability in the scores). More than one person must "see" or report the data in the same way (20 percent of the data in each phase is the standard, but we have a full chapter dedicated to this topic later in the book).

Finally, the more times you can "demonstrate" the effect, the more believable your conclusions will be. Three replications is the standard. Other standards include the length of the phases or how many data points. This is hotly debated but a generally accepted standard is five data points, although nine is a substantial improvement and better for determining trend and stability and chance. Other issues with conclusion validity include the consistency of the data: level, trend and variability (more on this later).

Main Components of Single Case Research

Single case research identifies a variable for study, measures that variable in one condition and compares it to another or others. The measurement and design of the study are critical components to a quality work and the difference between evidence for a practice and none. SCR can also be used for routine low stakes decisions where less stringent criteria are needed. Single case research is time series data, where an independent variable is systematically manipulated in order to determine the effect on a dependent variable and repeated measures are used to determine behavior change. Many design options exist; AB, ABAB, ABC, and multiple baselines are most common. Cause or functional relationships are determined in the design whereas the size of the change is a judgment about context (Socially valid? Meaningful to a client?). Finally, single case research is the study of an individual and individual target behaviors. In the remaining chapters of this book we will review each of the issues related to SCR design and analysis. The book is designed to be somewhat self-contained in the chapter organization, so if you know a lot about design but only a little about reliability or effect sizes, you can move to the chapters you need and skim or skip those you don't.

2

FOUNDATIONS OF SCR DESIGN AND VISUAL ANALYSIS

This chapter is designed to review research designs, portray the logic associated with the designs so that you can determine when to employ which design based on the questions they can answer and the needs of the student. There are essential ingredients that should be present in every design or are needed to use SCR regardless of student needs. Without these essential ingredients, the design is "broken" and therefore not useful for conclusions of any kind.

> *Science is the great antidote to the poison of enthusiasm and superstition.*
> (Adam Smith, *The Wealth of Nations*, 1863)

Research Designs and Their Logic

Single case research designs are intended for basic and applied research to answer questions about individual problems, or to develop theory. Prior to the Greeks (somewhere around the sixth century) no one was too concerned with a rational or "ordered" explanation of the universe, much less human behavior. Although Franklin, Allison, and Gorman (1997) provide an interesting account of early standardized measurement development in Chinese culture in 1115 BC (Wainer, 1990) and performance testing by Gideon in the old testament (Judges 7: 1–8).

The logic of SCR is characterized by a philosophical belief that the universe is ordered and observable phenomena become understandable when patterns are accurately identified. This empowers us to speculate and "predict" human behavior. These observations contribute to a unified system of knowledge. Rather than isolated events, all reasoning combines into a "reality." It is this reality we seek in the application of SCR to problems in school settings. How can we scientifically, rather than superstitiously account for the behavior of children, and how can we influence that behavior to improve educational outcomes and quality of life. Improved skill sets in children and youth as a result of scientific inquiry does not indicated a manipulated individual but rather a student more equipped for success and decision making.

Unlike group research where one group serves as a control for another group receiving treatment, in SCR the individual serves as "control" for themselves. The baseline condition is this control condition. When effects of variables are under question, the difference between the baseline condition and any subsequent treatment conditions should be confined to only the treatment or dependent variable. The introduction of extraneous variables means that other events could be responsible for change. So baseline and the description of baseline is an important first step in SCR. Baseline is not a condition to be handled sloppily as one "waits" to start treatment, but rather a carefully described environment and measured behaviors with as much control as is possible.

For example, Randy whistles in class to the distraction of teachers and others. Before we begin a program to change whistling, we need to know more about the current level, type, or degree of whistling behavior Randy exhibits, or we will not be able to measure the change. We also need to know what else is happening in the classroom so that we can maintain these other conditions when an intervention is begun.

In a baseline condition (control or no treatment) the target behavior whistling is measured. The measure could be duration (how long does the whistling occur) or frequency (how often does whistling happen) or perhaps intensity (how loudly or with what level of vigor). In addition to measuring whistling, we may also want to describe or measure any related events like the setting, the instruction, the frequency and type of interactions or task demands and or the proximity of relevant people like a teacher or other students. For if any of these things change, when treatment in introduced, more than the intervention has changed the environment and thus more than just the intervention should be investigated, or there are extraneous factors which may or may not account for change.

Consider this example: baseline whistling occurs at a level of X (let's say five times an hour for about 30 seconds each time). Intervention occurs and whistling is reduced to two times an hour and for only ten seconds each time. Was the intervention effective? From this look at the data one might say yes it was. Consider other environmental factors not described here, though. What if I say that in baseline, the teacher used worksheets and during intervention the class was engaged in group projects? Was the intervention responsible for the whistling change or was it the change in instructional task demands? Describing, measuring and reporting an environmental condition (and maintaining everything except the treatment) is a feature of a strong SCR study. More on this later when we discuss proximal and distal measures, but we want to introduce the concept now for your consideration.

Now let's take a look at the type of data we might collect on the behavior of interest—whistling. Repeated measures over time provide the following data. For the purpose of illustration (see Figure 2.1) we show data for three possible measures (duration, frequency, vigor). Reviewing the duration data we see stable data across Monday, Tuesday, Wednesday, and Thursday. The data is described as stable

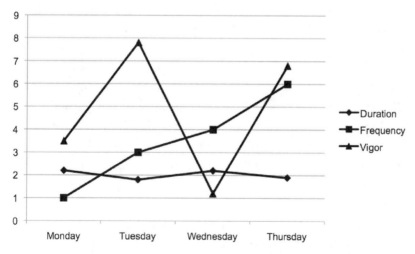

Figure 2.1 **Three types of measures for the same behavior.**

because it is relatively flat, there are no wide swings in data points, nor are there dramatic trends. Frequency data however is not stable. It shows an increasing trend, and vigor data although not trended is not stable.

Reliable measurement is critical for SCR designs. Counting is the most straightforward measure, but often a frequency will not capture the behavior. In the prior whistling example, notice that the frequency or count of whistling increased dramatically from Monday to Thursday. Was the behavior getting worse? If you were counting increases you might think "Yes," but looking at duration we see that the length of time spent whistling didn't change much at all, and the difference may be negligible if the Y axis represents minutes. Determining what and how to measure is an essential ingredient in SCR and these questions are informed by the target problem.

Essential Ingredients

Using SCR to solve problems in schools requires distinct essential ingredients: clients in need, identified target behaviors, appropriate measures and effective, or believed to be effective treatments.

Clients in Need

What is a client in need and who decides? I frequently joke with the expression that "I need an IEP (individual education plan)" for any number of my less-than-ideal behaviors—staying up too late, eating too many cookies, overzealous shoe shopping—you get the idea. Where, however, is the threshold of "need"? In school or school-related settings and applied SCR we typically draw the line at the level of educational need, for example when a child's grades are falling below a passing level, or when a behavior is causing removal from instructional time or otherwise interfering with learning. Clearly we consider the need to be "real" when a behavior is dangerous to the child or to others in the child's environment. There are instances, however, when determining whether or not a child is in need is a judgment call of the school team and parents or caregivers. This frequently is determined by examining the behaviors in question.

The following are sources that can be used for identification of problem behavior:

- *IEP/BIP goals*   By monitoring IEP/BIP goals, a teacher will be ready to show evidence of a student's progress towards goals at group decision-making meetings.
- *Teacher Selected Behaviors*   Sometimes, teachers have behavior concerns not addressed by the student's IEP/BIP goals. In this case, it may be useful to select behaviors that a teacher feels are most important to the student's education.
- *Parent Behavior Concerns*   Integrating parent concerns with goals identified at school, helps connect home and school in the goal of improving student behavior.
- *School Rules*   A review of past behavioral data and office referrals can be used to determine if the student has continuously violated the same school rules.
- *Functional Behavior Assessment*   Use this data to determine if typical behavior interferes with the physical, emotional, social and/or academic wellness of the student.

Target Behaviors

The first ingredient is a problem to solve or a target behavior, or a phenomenon under examination. Defining an individual behavioral goal is selecting key behaviors or behavior constellations (a group of related behaviors which occur together). Improvements in these behaviors or behavior constellations would significantly impact the quality of the student's school progress and life. How are these targets identified?

Social validity is one criterion. The behavior target should be meaningful to teachers and students, not just one or the other. If pencil tapping is tremendously annoying to a teacher, but not interfering with a student's learning then perhaps this behavior is less valid for change. The targeting of a behavior should reflect and respect culture and cultural differences or preferences. There is a difference between cultural sensitivity and cultural competency. A team determining a behavior to target should seek clear understanding of cultural beliefs prior to targeting behavior. Targets should reflect behavioral expectations of the school and classroom as well however, and it is desirable for these last two concepts to not be at odds with each other. Ideally target behaviors are valued or seen as important overall in that improvement would make a sizeable difference in quality of student's life or school career. Finally, target behavior should reflect age or grade normative behaviors.

Practicality is another criterion. The target should be the next logical step in improvement or the change needed in the student. In order to work well in this type of scientific paradigm and for repeated measures, the behavior is expected to be observed and measured most days rather than be a behavior that is a very rare event. Fighting on the playground for example, would be difficult to measure frequently and often in most instances, whereas on-task/off-task behavior is likely to occur with great regularity and frequency. The behavior is expected to be "changeable" or within the possible repertoire of the individual. Some bio-physical or physiological problems cannot be changed regardless of home and school interventions. Given effective interventions, change should be visible over a short to medium time period. Finally, the behavior should such that a reliable measure is obtainable, that is, not impossible.

To be reliably measured, behavior should be directly observable. To do this we avoid inferring student motives, intentions, or feelings. Most commonly this behavior is measureable through countables (frequency, duration, latency) or qualitative indicators (behavioral descriptions).

The more well defined the behavior is, the more accurate the measurement. For example, most people would likely describe whistling in a similar way or be able to reliably recognize whistling, but what about aggression or distraction? These are more difficult constructs to agree on, so clear examples and non-examples are helpful for observers when identifying the behavior. The way behavior is identified for change, or the way a problem is conceptualized will affect the type of measurement you will take and should be under consideration when designing the measures.

Consider the following three examples for aggression (see Figure 2.2). The identified behaviors dictate, to an extent, the type(s) of measures you need. Measurement of aggression—the *construct*—is not

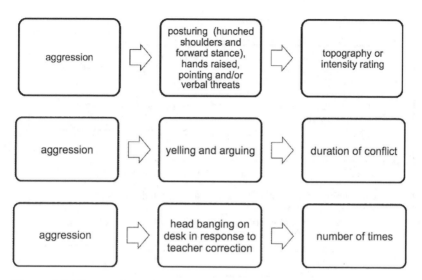

Figure 2.2 **Illustration of three types of behavioral problems for the same construct.**

the likely candidate for frequent repeated measures, but the secondary description of its *manifestation* is ideal for that.

Appropriate Measures

A third essential ingredient is appropriate measurement. This ingredient is informed by the target behavior in question—the "what" you are going to measure—but Figure 2.3 shows some options which can be used alone or in tandem with other measures.

There are additional considerations for the measure you determine is best and those considerations are related to the sensitivity with which you can detect changes in behavior and the degree of exactness with which you need to measure the behavior.

Take the following example: Jack engages in a variety of problem behaviors one of which is elopement. He periodically runs from the classroom. Sometimes Jack side steps to the door with his head down as though he can't be seen. Sometimes he will bolt to the door and stop and laugh, other times Jack will run out of the door and down the hall. Once out of the classroom, Jack may laugh out loud and touch bulletin boards as he zigzags down the hall or he may just run and hide.

Frequency

- Frequency is the counting or occurance of a behavior. Frequency can be divided by time and transformed into a ratio for comparison when intervals for measurment are unequal.
- for example the number of times Keshawn rocks back in his chair or the number of times Missi asks for help by shouting out rather than raising her hand.

Duration

- Duration is the length of time from start to finish of a behavior. Duration is useful for low incidence, longer lasting episodes or when behavior is complicated and changing but the construct of interst remains the same.
- for example the duration of a tantrum, which might include yelling, falling to the ground and/or refusing to participate.

Latency

- Latency is the length of time between two events.
- for example a teacher asks Jacob to stop talking. The length of time between the request and Jacob's compliance is latency.

Intensity

- Intensity is the degree or strength of a behavior.
- for example Phu-le refuses to go to the bathroom and cries to avoid compliance. The intensity of the crying would be measured using a scale.

Ratings or Scales

- Ratings or rating scales use categories with names or numbers to represent the categories.
- For example, Always Sometimes Never is a 3 point scale or A,B,C,D, F is a 5 point scale.

Figure 2.3 **Measurement options.**

A frequency count will not capture enough detail about Jack's behavior nor would duration or latency. Intensity or a topographical description added to a scale is likely the best method to measure this behavior set as it is not easily operationalized to fit in count data. What type of scale should we use, though?

A scale is an ordered set of judgments of levels of behavior quality, with numbers attached to the levels. Scaling is the process of seg-

menting quality or quantity of behavior into an ordered set of categories (three, four, five or up to ten is reasonable), from least to most
desirable. Movement across the scale reflects improvement toward
meeting a behavioral goal. The more categories in the scale, the more
sensitivity in detecting change. A "yes/no" measure provides less
sensitivity than a 1–10 rating. If you picture the Y axis on a graph you
can visualize the difference. This example shows the difference
between a 1–10 range for scoring elopement (Figure 2.4) and a simple
"yes/no" (Figure 2.5). You can infer from this example why scales
about following school rules may not be best as a "yes/no".

What about scales that aren't as easy to count? How do I create a
scale for that type of measurement? Take a look at the following two
examples.

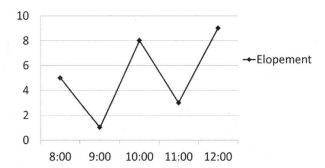

Figure 2.4 **Illustration of measurement sensitivity: Scaling behavior
on a ten-point scale in comparison to a two-point scale.**

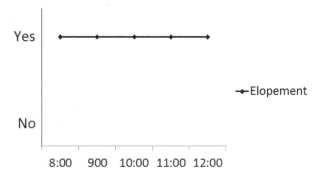

Figure 2.5 **Example illustrating the same data using a Yes/No scale.**

*Issue 1: Maintaining "On-task" Behavior Using an
Estimation/Approximation Scale*

Mrs. Kalis is frustrated with Leo's "disruptive behaviors" during instruction. She considers "disruption" to mean: wandering around or bothering other students, and/ or speaking too loudly when working with peers.

- *Scaling Issue*: Mrs. Kalis would like to start a referral for special services. Her school asks her to take data on Leo's behavior during class but Mrs. Kalis is unsure if she can take data on all these problems and still manage and teach her class. The team creates an estimation scale with no counting (see Table 2.1).

*Issue 2: Inappropriate Verbal Interactions Using
a Qualitative Judgment Scale*

Mrs. Romo and Mr. Johnson have concerns about Angel sleeping during labs, arriving late and sometimes missing the 1st period class completely.

Table 2.1 **Illustration of an A-F scale for topography of disruptive behavor**

Behavior	Indicator				
	A	B	C	D	F
Failure to stay in his seat, bothering other students, and/or keep his voice quiet when working with peers.	In seat, cooperative and appropriate voice 99% of the class time.	In seat, cooperative, and appropriate voice 85–99% of the class time	In seat, cooperative, and appropriate voice 75–85% of the class time	Any combination of out of seat, bothering other students, using loud voice when working with peers. Between 25–50% of the class.	Any combination of out of seat, bothering other students, using a loud voice when working with peers. More than 1/2 of the class.

Table 2.2 **Illustration of a 5 point scale**

Behavior	Indicator				
	1	*2*	*3*	*3*	*4*
Sleeping in class or lab	Awake all of the class or lab time.	Awake but appears sleepy or is struggling to stay awake.	Falls asleep during class, eyes may be red or under eyes dark.	Arrives tardy to class.	Is absent from class.

- *Scaling Issue*: Teachers are concerned with the sleeping and also the cause of the sleeping so the team creates a scale to capture the problem in a way that may be useful for a doctor or parent as well as the team. (see Table 2.2).

Notice in this example that the numbers are reversed so that when graphing the "high" point on the graphic display will be the appropriate behavior and the "low" point on the graph will be the less desirable behavior. This allows improvement to be represented as "up" movement and although this technical detail is not critical, representing "up" as desired and "down" as not is sometimes more interpretable. If you are scaling a problem behavior, then the reverse would be true and you would want to show progress as a downward trend as problem behavior decreased.

Effective, or Believed to be Effective Treatments

Treatments or interventions (although not the topic of this book) are expected to be employed to remedy the problem for the client and outcomes measured to determine effects. Remember that efficacy is whether or not a treatment "works" under ideal conditions. Effectiveness is whether or not something works in a real world environment. As a field we are expected to use efficacious treatments (those things which have evidence to support their use). With individual clients in "messy" real world settings, however, results are sometimes difficult to replicate. So in addition to using evidence-based practices, we are compelled to take good measures to determine their effects across settings and clients. There are many sources for evidence-based practices and the number and available evidence grows each year. Consider the *What Works Clearing House* by the Department of Education (Kratochwill et al., 2010), or texts such as *The Intervention Guide* (Vannest, Reynolds, & Kamphaus, 2008) or the *Handbook of Research on EBD* (Rutherford, Quinn, & Mathur, 2004). In addition some specific papers on interventions for individuals on the autistic spectrum can be found by reading work by J. Ganz and colleagues.

Experimental Design Options

- *Reversal designs* or ABAB designs demonstrate experimental control by introducing treatment (A1–B1) reversing treatment effects (B1–A2), and reintroducing treatment (A2–B2). This design is appropriate for answering questions about the effect of a treatment when the effect can be reversed. For example: "What is the effect of guided notes on attention during lecture?" or "What is the effect of Adderall(tm) on hyperactivity during sustained silent reading?" The more correct terminology is withdrawal however (Kennedy, 2005) because withdrawal does not suggest or presuppose the effect will reverse (Leitenberg, 1973) whereas the term reversal (Baer, Wolf, & Risley, 1968) does appear to suggest this a priori decision.

The idea of "reversibility" is sometimes more obvious than at other times. We would assume "walking" to have a low-probability of reversal. Likewise "reading" would be unlikely to reverse, but what about attention, or disruptive behavior? Once an individual learns a new technique or skill will that skill be engaged in a manner to prevent reversal? When does reversal "not occur" demonstrating a lack of effect or "not occur" demonstrating a learned behavior? Professional decision making and clear data in context are useful in making this determination. BAB is a variant of this design, but one in which the intervention condition "starts" first. There are legitimate reasons for this design related to the needs of the client, for example the intervention is already in place.

- *Alternating treatments and multi-component designs* compare one treatment condition to another against a baseline of no treatment. These designs are useful when a multi-component package intervention is used or when elements responsible for behavior change in particular are difficult to determine. An alternating treatment design could include a layer or additional treatment when the B phase does not produce the intended effect.
- *Multiple baseline designs* are useful when it is expected that behaviors will not reverse or when it is unethical to reverse a treatment, under these circumstances experimental control is demonstrated by replication across participants or behaviors or settings. The use of a self-monitoring wrist watch timer to prevent soiling could be used for Tom, Estella, and Tulane. The intervention (wrist watch timer) would be introduced sequentially by allowing the baseline to extend for each subsequent participant. An intervention of graphic organizers could be introduced for one participant across classes of History, Geography, and Language Arts. An intervention of "precorrection" could be introduced for Timothy for behaviors of laughing to himself, pulling out eyebrows, and swaying while waiting in line.
- *Considerations for length of baseline* An issue related to baseline stability then is how much data is required to determine stability? Barlow and Hersen (1973) suggested three points as a sufficient baseline. This guideline was reinforced in later influential texts by these authors (Hersen & Barlow 1976, 1984) but Parsonson & Baer (1992) called five data points an excessively short baseline. Others do not make static recommendations for number of data points necessary for a base line, and instead raise concerns about trend (Kazdin, 1982; 2010; Kratochwill, 2010), however in practice, the questions which arise are regarding the number of data points that constitute a necessary and sufficient baseline.

Sidman (1960) qualified baseline stability as a range of 5 percent (or less) variability in behavior. Simkins, nine years later provides a caveat that although stability is the ideal, practical considerations in psychological endeavors mean that we do not have the ability to control the environment in order to obtain a baseline with 5 percent or less variability. Baer, Wolf, and Risley (1968), recommended that the baseline should be extended until "stability is clear," however clarity was not objectified. Tawney and Gast (1984) also indicate to wait until stability is achieved before introducing intervention. Similarly, Pawlicki (1970) recommended that a baseline is stable when a sufficient period of time has passed so as to attain reliability. Ironically he reported fewer than one-third of behavior-therapy studies with children between 1965 and 1969 report a stable baseline (n = 54). The concept of stability in baseline has always been viewed as an important consideration (Sidman, 1960; Hersen & Barlow 1976, 1984; Kazdin, 1982) however the specification of stability has not been evaluated empirically.

In a random sample of published SCR designs, Vannest and Parker found that 31 of the 374 datasets contained only four baseline data points. Three data points cannot be judged reliably and you cannot predict the rest of baseline based on just three data points, even when stable. Recording four, five or six data points is not much better unless your baseline is completely stable. Any trend or variability in the data introduces a tremendous source of error. As a general rule, five stable baseline data points (meaning a variation of less than 10 percent) may be enough. Variability in baseline data would call for nine or more data points to reliably represent behavior and would suggest the need to revisit environmental control considerations.

Visual Analysis

Some experts have contended that visual analysis should be the sole or at least primary method for single-case design data (Baer, 1977; Michael, 1974; Parsonson & Baer, 1978, 1986), arguing that visual analysis will reveal any intervention effects large enough to be important to clinicians. They argue that visual analysis yields low error rates (Huitema, 1986) and is conservative in identifying treatment effects (Baer, 1977), and therefore that the increased sensitivity which statistical analyses may offer is not needed (Parsonson & Baer, 1986).

Despite these perceived strengths of visual analysis, even its strong advocates tend to recommend statistical analysis as a supplement in some cases. Kazdin (1982) stated that statistical procedures may be of value when: (a) there is no stable baseline, (b) expected treatment effects cannot be well-predicted, as with a new treatment, (c) statistical control is needed for extraneous factors in naturalistic environments. Huitema (1986), also a strong supporter of visual analysis, recommends supplemental statistical analyses when unambiguous results must be shared with other professionals. Franklin, Gorman, Beasley, and Allison (1997) conclude a recent book chapter on the subject by emphasizing the need to integrate visual and statistical analyses. White, Rusch, Kazdin, and Hartmann (1989) acknowledge that the "logic of decision making that underlies single-case investigations is compatible with statistical reasoning" (p. 283). They say that the challenge is to develop statistical tests that are sensitive and sophisticated enough to reflect complex judgments of the research.

Reliability of Visual Analysis

Considerable evidence has been amassed which casts doubt on the reliability of judgments made from visual analyses. Several studies inquiring into the reliability of visual judgments have consistently found low to moderate interrater reliabilities, in the 0.40–0.60 range (DeProspero & Cohen, 1979; Harbst, Ottenbacher, & Harris, 1991; Ottenbacher, 1990; Park, Marascuilo, & Gaylord-Ross, 1990). Park, Marascuilo, and Gaylord-Ross (1990) found that even among expert raters, interrater agreements were 27 percent for graphs with statistically significant results, and 67 percent for graphs without significant results. In addition, Harbst et al. (1991) found that journal reviewers performed little better than untrained raters at graph judgment tasks.

Graphic features have occasionally been modified to help increase the reliability of visual analysis judgments. Trend lines have been added to help increase the reliability and validity of visual analysis-based ratings. Results, however, have not been uniformly positive. Instead, the trend lines sometimes created dependencies, helped maintain inconsistent judgments, and led to overemphasis on trend to the neglect of other features (DeProspero & Cohen, 1979; Greenspan & Fisch, 1992; Hojem & Ottenbacher, 1988; Skiba et al., 1989).

The effect of training on visual analysis also has been examined. Wampold and Furlong (1981) compared judgments on 36 AB graphs by small groups of students trained in visual analysis with those trained in multivariate analysis. Even extensive training produced only small changes in judgment, although training in multivariate techniques proved superior in getting students to attend to small variations across phases. Harbst et al. (1991) also found that student training in single-subject research had little influence on visual analysis judgments.

Confounds to Visual Analysis

Another current criticism of visual analysis is based on mounting evidence that visual analysis is confounded by the same data attributes as is statistical analysis, for example autocorrelation, data cyclicity, and pre-existing linear trend (Allison, 1992; Greenwald, 1976; Jones, Weinrott, & Vaught, 1978; Keppel, 1982). Matyas and Greenwood (1990) found that Type I (false positives) error rates from visual judgments tend to be positively related to autocorrelation. With no autocorrelation, Type I error rate ranged from 0 to approximately 13 percent, but the error rate raised to 16 percent–84 percent with autocorrelation present. Jones, Weinrott, and Vaught (1978) also found that autocorrelation substantially reduced the validity of visual analysis, that is, its agreement with statistical analysis. With moderate-to-high serial dependency, visual analysis judgments were reduced to nearly chance levels.

Validation Research on Visual Analysis

Given that judgments from visual analysis tend to possess low–moderate reliabilities, they cannot be expected to produce high validity coefficients, and such has been the case, typically yielding coefficients of 0.37 to 0.55 (Harbst et al., 1991). Of greater concern, however, is the quality of the several criterion-related validity studies conducted to date on visual analysis-based judgments. Most have marked inadequacies, namely unrealistic visual analysis conditions and the use of questionable external criteria. Parsonson and Baer (1992) indicate that these problems began with the earliest visual analysis research (Jones et al., 1978), and, for the most part, have continued to the present (Matyas & Greenwood, 1990).

In real world practice, visual analysis: (a) considers the context of a particular client and intervention, (b) makes use of multiple interacting data characteristics (variability, mean levels, trends, intercepts) both within and across phases, (c) draws conclusions of practical signifi-cance (magnitude of treatment effect, not p values), and (d) draws conclusions about amount or degree of effectiveness (not "yes/no" judgements) (Parsonson & Baer, 1992). Most visual analysis validity studies, however: (a) present decontextualized data, (b) require a respondent to judge a single statistical parameter (usually mean or slope difference), (c) require respondents to identify a significant p value level for the statistic, and (d) require respondents to make dichotomous "yes/no" decisions (Furlong & Wampold, 1982; Rojahn & Schulze, 1985; Wampold & Furlong, 1981). With respect to presentation of decontextualized graphs, judges have complained about this problem, some refusing to participate for this very reason (DeProspero & Cohen, 1979; Knapp, 1983).

Different Validation Criteria Produce Different Results

Another limitation of most visual analysis validation studies is that the criterion measure—usually a statistic—is poorly defined or is, itself, questionable. Parsonson and Baer (1992) state "there is no single process called statistical analysis to provide that putative standard or truth; there are many of them, which in their diversity often allow quite different conclusions" (p. 21). For example, there are at least four common methods of calculating mean level shift: (a) simple mean difference, (b) mean difference controlling for overall data trend in the response variable (semipartial correlation), (c) mean difference controlling for overall trend in both response and predictor variables (partial correlation), and (d) mean difference controlling for baseline trend only. Which of these five is selected as the standard for judging visual analysis will greatly affect results. Nourbakhsh and Ottenbacher (1994) found that three supposedly very similar statistical indices (C statistic, two-standard deviation band method, "split middle" method) actually performed very differently when applied to the same set of data. The warning from past research is clear: multiple validation criteria should be used for a clear understanding of visual analysis judgments.

Moreover, existing studies suffer from ambiguity in how judges are directed to respond. One problematic example is by Jones, et al. (1978) who asked raters to judge AB graphs for "reliable change in level," yet both terms "reliable" and "change in level" are undefined and problematic. "Level" may refer to any of: (a) a change in mean level, (b) the difference in trend line intercepts at intervention onset, or (c) the difference between the last baseline data point and first treatment data point (very transient) (Parsonson & Baer, 1992).

In addition, studies which have used only a small number of graphs (for example, Ottenbacher, 1986; Ottenbacher, 1990) confound the effects of mean differences, trend differences, autocorrelation and intercept level differences at intervention onset. So judgments of one type of effect are likely influenced by other effects as well. Mean shift will commonly accompany trend shift and jumps in intercept level, and may also accompany changes in variability. We have learned in recent years that mean and trend differences also are commonly confounded with autocorrelation (Gibson & Ottenbacher, 1988). Thus, most published visual analysis research has been badly flawed.

Visual Analysis Considerations

- *Variability* is the degree of change in the data. Variability is the antithesis of stability (see discussion above on baseline). Variability, also known as bounce, is a threat to internal validity and represents either unstable behavior (truly) or a lack of control in the environment. The assumption of variability, scientifically, is that if an environment is held constant and all stimuli or antecedents and consequences to behavior are constant, then behavior should also be predictable. Some scenarios indicate that behavior may swing radically and the range of performance represents the "true" behavior.

- *Trend* The use of a trend line to measure improvement in data has a long history. Since short time series data typically do not meet the data assumptions necessary to apply parametric methods (Parker, 2006), visual analysts have made efforts to show summative trend in data without using regression based techniques. Wald's (1940) seminal article described early efforts to create trend lines through paper and pencil techniques. Several of the simple "robust" methods which have stood the test of time are summarized by Hoaglin, Mosteller, and Tukey, (1983). The various methods are similar, but have some key differences. First, the data on the X axis are sectioned vertically into halves (Brown & Mood, 1951; Wald, 1940) or thirds (Bartlett, 1949; Gibson & Jowett, 1957; Tukey, 1977). Then lines are drawn through either means (Bartlett, 1949; Gibson & Jowett, 1957; Wald, 1940) or medians (Brown & Mood, 1951; Tukey, 1977; White, 1987) of sectioned data. Mean or median X and Y values are obtained for each section, and the points of intersection are used either to calculate a "line of best fit" or to draw a line of best fit with a ruler.

These methods have long been used by visual analysts to judge improvement; however, no empirical studies have evaluated how much data is necessary to show a reliable trend or improvement beyond chance level. Vannest and Parker found in a reliable visual analysis of trend that of 374 data sets, 339 (90 percent) had clear, visually identifiable data level change or lack of stability. Later we will teach and discuss statistical methods for addressing trend, as trend is common but perfect trend is not, and thus short time series data tend to be unpredictable making judgments about effects difficult under most circumstances.

- *Mean or median levels* are the averages or the level of most common "score" or data point for each phase. A comparison of mean or level changes is sometimes used to determine the effect of an intervention. This gets into issues of overlapping data, stability and trend which we have discussed already and will later learn methods to better assess the size of a change.
- *Intercept gap* is the change in behavior demonstrated between phases. When A phase is finished and B phase is introduced the

"gap" between A and B should be pronounced and large if the intervention has a strong and immediate effect. There are times when an intercept gap will not be so pronounced. For example when the effects of treatment are cumulative or when a "training phase" is not parceled out and there is a learning curve to understanding or using the intervention technique.

3

SCR STATISTICAL ANALYSIS

In an era of accountability with a focus on the defensibility of employed practices and their outcomes, there are many purposes for the statistical analysis of SCR. These include identifying evidence-based practices to adopt, defending instructional or programmatic decisions for individual clients or students, and instructional decision making. In previous chapters we have identified the visual analysis skills, guidelines and techniques necessary for evaluating data but visual analysis are not always sufficient.

- *Case example 1* Jill is a seventh-grader struggling in academics and behavior, her schedule includes both general education and special education classroom settings and instruction. Teachers take daily data on Jill's performance in academics and behavior. Six is the highest (best) rating and zero is the lowest (worst) rating, A score of three is considered "typical seventh grader" as an anchor. Six is superior and zero is critical. The teachers take data in their respective classes for four days before starting an intervention (see Figure 3.1 below). Then they begin a "check in check out" type of intervention where each teacher has agreed to greet Jill at the door with a smile and hello or "fist bump" type encouragement. At the end of each class, Jill brings her tablet to the teacher who rates her on her academic and social behavior. This includes paying attention, asking questions, responding to answers, compliance with teacher requests and not distracting others. All of which have been explained to Jill with modeling, practice and Jill demonstrating an understanding and awareness of her own behaviors. When the team meets to review the effects of this intervention and whether or

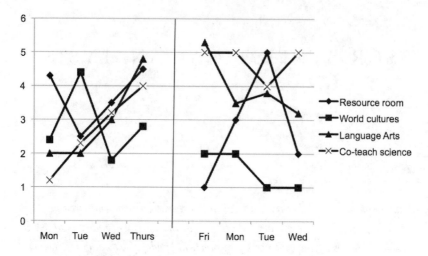

Figure 3.1 **Ratings of Jill's academic and social behavior.**

not to train the other teachers and continue the practice they have the following graphed data.

Visually it is somewhat clear that the intervention had problems in world cultures class and this could be discussed to determine if it was implemented well and what happened in this scenario. It may seem to the team that the practice was effective in the co-teach Science but a close inspection of the baseline data shows a significant positive trend in the data. The effects in Language Arts and the resource room are visually unclear. This data is not atypical in school settings where environments are not scientifically controlled and implementation is sometimes less than ideal. If this data is going to be useful to a team for instructional decision making or defending educational placement decisions, more information is needed about the size of the behavior change.

   There are many statistical analysis of SCR that can be used to determine an effect size and the confidence intervals (the certainty of the decision). The level of difficulty in these calculations is in direct proportion to their sophistication. Before we begin to review and lay out how to do these analyses, we would like to first share with you the methods we will not review and why.

There are four common categories of analysis for data. Two are parametric analysis procedures and include regression and multi-level models. These are methods typically seen for large data sets and they require certain properties of the data in order to be accurate. Non-parametric methods also exist such as the non-overlap techniques. So that you are a fully knowledgeable consumer we will briefly summarize some pros and cons of these techniques.

Regression models have assumptions about the score scale and data distribution which SCR data rarely meets. Regression assumes linear trend and in order for these methods to work, the autocorrelation of the data must be cleansed or modeled in some way. This is unlikely to work in a school setting. Regression has much to offer however and we are not opposed to its use, but rather have identified a variety of limitations. On the positive side, regression is flexible, has a strong history of use and is visually accessible (plots of model fit lines).

Multi-Level Models are a "black box" to all but the statistically sophisticated. These are not "visually accessible" and so for most we cannot critique the model or how it is used because we are not privy to the very complex model. In addition MLM (multi-level models) are bound by unique assumptions which have not yet been tested. As such, there is really no "history of use." MLM generally require larger Ns (sample size) than in a single study, however, MLM voids the assumptions that trip up regression (including serial independence) and MLM can fit both nonparametric and parametric models. MLM is really set up for the summary of large data sets.

Randomization Models do not typically work with smaller designs. These models work best with a design which has many short phases. Most difficult in a school context, randomization models place demands on random assignment of treatments and clients which most interventionists would not accept. This model could be used in determining a best practice but would require extensive controls in the assignment of treatments. Trend sensitivity is problematic and should be monitored. This model yields a p-value, not an effect size, however this method like MLM avoid the assumptions that trip up regression (including serial independence).

Dominance (Non-overlap) Models can lack sensitivity in discriminating strongest and weakest effects. So comparing effects between treatments that are both very strong or both very weak would be difficult. Dominance models have somewhat less power than other regression models. This technique is also blind to trend in both baseline and intervention phases. It is, however, "distribution free," making minimal assumptions about score scale or data distribution. Furthermore these models are highly compatible with visual analysis, and with hand calculations they offer confidence intervals, p-values and reasonable power.

The number and quality of statistical techniques for SCR have dramatically increased in the last decade and there are currently ten published nonparametric methods in the literature. We would like to list those here for you but we will review and provide step by step instructions only for those we feel are your best bets for use in schools. This is based on the use and analysis of hundreds of SCR data sets (Parker, Vannest, & Davis, 2011; A review of Nine Overlap Methods in Behavior Modification). One of these methods is the Improvement Rate Difference or IRD (Parker, Vannest & Brown, 2009). IRD is the difference in behavior between phase A and phase B. IRD first appeared in the medical literature as "risk reduction" using the difference of two proportions. IRD is calculated from a two-by-two table (see Figure 3.2).

The first step in IRD is to eliminate all data overlap. We do this by identifying the minimum number of data points needing removal. With each data point removed, check the graph to see if any overlap remains. For example, if two data are on the same Y value, only one (not both) need to be removed to eliminate overlap. In this example (Figure 3.3) there are two data points which overlap (Friday in phase A, and Wednesday in phase B). One, not both data points need removing to eliminate the overlap.

In most instances there will be more than one data point needing removal to eliminate overlap. Eliminate the *fewest* possible number of data points. To make the analysis most robust, the removal of data should be split between A and B phases to balance the table. In the Refusal to Comply example there are four data points which "overlap"

Group

	Intervention	Baseline	Totals
Improv.	*(a)*	*(b)*	
No Improv.	*(c)*	*(d)*	
Totals	*(a+c)*	*(b+d)*	

Figure 3.2 **2 × 2 table.**

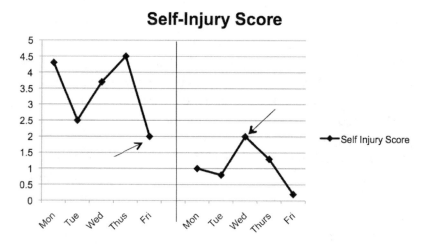

Figure 3.3 **IRD example.**

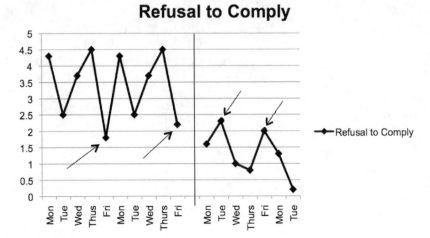

Figure 3.4 **Second IRD example.**

(Figure 3.4). Eliminating two data points from either side, both in phase A or both in phase B would eliminate the overlap, however, this would be "unbalanced" so whenever possible (and in this example) remove one data point from A and one from B, rather than both from each side.

Removing Friday in phase A and Tuesday in phase B eliminates all overlap and splits the removal equally between A and B. See the large circles as the "removal" to demonstrate the elimination of overlap.

The number of data points removed are called "improved." To calculate the improvement rate for each phase divide the number of data points remaining by the number of data points originally in the phase. In phase A there are ten data points, one is removed so 1/10 or 10 percent. In phase B there are seven data points originally and one is removed so 1/7 = 14 percent. IRD is the difference between these two rates. The size of the change in behavior is 15 percent (90–85). IRD also equals Cohen's Kappa and Cramer's V (Cliff, 1993). If a confidence interval or p-value is desired, those can be calculated using any common statistics module testing the difference between two proportions.

Another analysis is the non-overlap of all pairs (NAP) (Parker & Vannest, 2009). NAP is the percent of data which show improvement

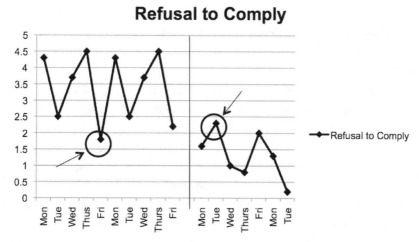

Figure 3.5 **Second IRD example highlighting overlap.**

from one phase to another based on all pairwise comparisons across phases A and B. NAP is calculated by scoring each pairwise comparison. An "improvement" is given a score of one, and a tie is a 0.5. Improvement here means data which increases or decreases in the direction desired. The "improvements" added to the "ties" is divided by the total number of pairs.

Hand calculation is a little tedious on long data sets but not unreasonably so:

1. Find the total number of paired comparisons by multiplying the number of data points in phase A and number of data points in phase B.
2. Identify the "overlap" zone by finding the lowest point in phase A and the highest point in phase B (if you are expecting behavior to decrease with treatment) or the reverse if appropriate. Count the pairs which show decline (Neg) and ties (Ties). These are subtracted from the number of pairs to obtain the number of "positives."
3. NAP at chance value is 50 percent so divide by 0.5 and subtract from one. If you want to use a statistics program, you will find this analysis in the Diagnostic Tests or ROC module using Area under the Curve.

Using Jill's data (Figure 3.6) let's walk through both IRD and NAP calculations. To calculate an effect size on a comparison of A and B phases, we will do each class separately. Data are shown below from an Excel worksheet (Table 3.1).

By examining the data lines for world cultures (as an example) we find the fewest number of data points needing removal in order to remove overlap is just one (third data point in phase A). By removing this data point we have eliminated the overlap of any data between A and B phases for world cultures. Next we calculate the "improvement rate." Phase A has 1/4 or 0.25 and phase B has 4/4 or 1.00. Subtracting the difference we have a 75 percent improvement rate difference. Here this is interpreted as deterioration because in this example we want Jill's academic and social performance to go up when in fact it got worse.

If I were to calculate NAP by hand, I would first calculate the number of paired comparisons by multiplying the number of data points in A and B. Using the world cultures data again we have four data points in A and four in B, so 16 pairwise comparisons are possible. Next I find the overlap zone. In this instance the three data points with a value of 1.8 in phase A, and 2. 2 in phase B would be the overlap zone. Compare the overlap data point in A with each of the B phase data with (see arrows in Figure 3.7). 1.8 and 2; 1.8 and 2; 1.8 and 1; 1.8 and 1. Data which is "improved" is scored as a one based on the

Table 3.1 Jill's data across days and subjects

Day	Subject			
	Resource room	World cultures	Language arts	Co-teach science
Mon	4.3	2.4	2	1.2
Tue	2.5	4.4	2	2.3
Wed	3.5	1.8	3	3.2
Thurs	4.5	2.8	4.8	4
Fri	1	2	5.3	5
Mon	3	2	3.5	5
Tue	5	1	3.8	4
Wed	2	1	3.2	5

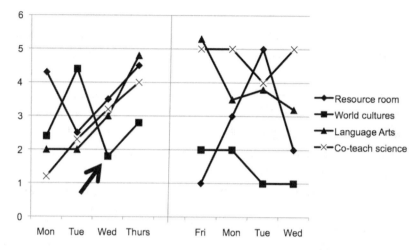

Figure 3.6 **Jill's data.**

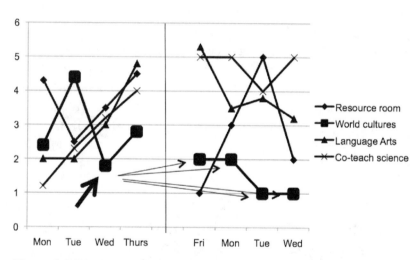

Figure 3.7 **World cultures data series, arrows illustrating NAP.**

pairwise comparison, data which is a tie is scored as 0.5, and data with no improvement is a zero. So these pair comparisons would give us a score of one, one, zero and zero, or a total of 2. Subtracting this number from the total number of possible pairs we get $16 - 2 = 14$, NAP $= 14/16$ or 0.87. This change in behavior should also be interpreted in the context of the behavior under study. In this instance the behavior has decreased 87 percent.

The difference in effect size (IRD=75 percent and NAP=87.5 percent) is due to relatively higher impact of removing a data point in the IRD equation. Since every data point is compared in the NAP calculation, the influence of the overlap is half of what it is in the IRD equation. that is, rather than removing 25 percent of data in IRD you remove 12.5 percent in NAP since the data point only overlaps with half of the phase B data. This is a reasonable example of the difference between the two calculation techniques and the influence of a single data point with small data sets.

If you wanted to do this equation (NAP) using a statistical package such as NCSS (Hintze, 2006) NAP is available as the area under the curve (AUC) percent from a ROC analysis. Go to Diagnostic tests, set actual condition variable to Phase, the Criterion variable to Scores, Positive Condition Value to B (phase B), Text Direction to High x Positive. Output is empirical AUS = 0.87).

Using the same data set to illustrate another example of IRD and NAP but this time using Language Arts data series (Figure 3.8). To calculate IRD, we first remove the data needed to eliminate all the overlap. The least number of data to be removed to eliminate overlap would be the fourth data point in phase A (see arrow). To make the calculation robust split the amount across both phases so 0.5 for each.

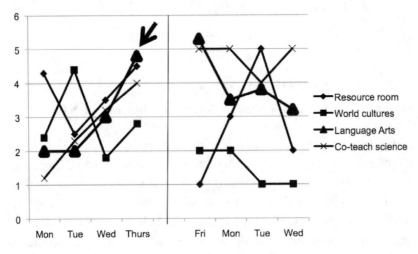

Figure 3.8 **Data series Language Arts example.**

The improvement rate for phase A is then 0.5 / 4 or 0.12 and for phase B it is four improved: 0.5 or 3.5 / 4 or 0.875. NAP is therefore 0.875 − 0.12 or 0.755 interpreted as a 75 percent change in behavior. Contextually we desired for academic and social behavior to improve so this is a gain in performance and a positive change.

To calculate NAP the possible pairs are four by four, or 16. We then compare the overlapping data point to each data point in the next phase. Thursday's data point in phase A has a value of 4.8 (see Table 3.2). A comparison of each pair would be 4.8 to 5.3, 4.8 to 3.5, 4.8 to 3.8 and 4.8 to 3.2. We score each as a one for improvement, 0.5 for a tie and zero for non-improvement. Scoring these pairs we have a 1, 0, 0, and 0.16 − 1 = 15 and 15/16 = 0.93 improvement.

Laura Leigh's daily performance in Chemistry is highly variable. The teacher has nearly two weeks of data to demonstrate that some days Laura brings her equipment, participates in labs and turns in assignments. Other days Laura barely lifts her head off the desk except to glare and cover her head with her LA Raiders hoodie. Using a mean or median score to reflect Laura Leigh's baseline performance would not reflect an accurate picture (See Figure 3.9).

Mean level comparisons only work well when means and standard deviations are an appropriate representation of the score distribution (Siegel & Castellan, 1988; Wilcox, 2010). Neither is a median a good reflection of scores typically found in SCR data (Scruggs &

Table 3.2 **Data from Language Arts example**

Day	Subject			
	Resource room	World cultures	Language arts	Co-teach science
Mon	4.3	2.4	2	1.2
Tue	2.5	4.4	2	2.3
Wed	3.5	1.8	3	3.2
Thurs	4.5	2.8	4.8	4
Fri	1	2	5.3	5
Mon	3	2	3.5	5
Tue	5	1	3.8	4
Wed	2	1	3.2	5

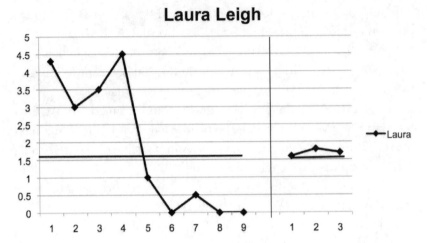

Figure 3.9 **Data illustrating mean summary for highly variable data.**

Mastropieri, 1998; 2001). Non-overlap methods do not rely on means, medians, or modes. Non-overlap techniques consider all data points in some comparison across phases. Most consider all data points equally. Exceptions are the original percent of non-overlapping data (PND) (Scruggs, Mastropieri, & Casto, 1987), which uses only one data point in phase A (the greatest value) and percentage of data points exceeding the mean (PEM) (Ma, 2006) and extended celeration line (ECL) (White & Haring, 1980) which both use a mix of non-overlap and median calculation. A non-overlap technique could tell us the size of the behavior change for Laura Leigh.

Another issue in selecting an SCR analysis method is the presence of positive baseline trend or trend which would obscure the results of treatment. For example, consider Stuart's data (Figure 3.10). Stuart's on-task behavior in his second-grade enrichment reading classroom shows steady progress. When the teacher does an interest inventory and adds books on airplanes, Stuart's on-task behavior increases. Calculating the effects of high-interest literature on "on-task" behavior should take into account his initial growth.

Stuart On-Task Behavior

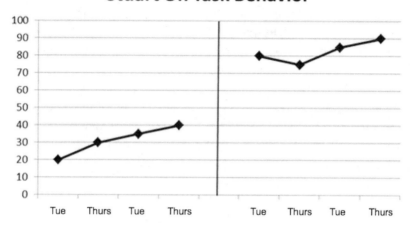

Figure 3.10 **Data set illustrating behavior change after intervention.**

Methods That Address Trend

When you determine that a baseline has a positive trend or a trend in the direction of the desired behavior change (that is, decreasing aggression) the analysis will ideally use a method which corrects for trend. This way, the effect you determine is more accurate because it is adjusted for the performances documented prior to the intervention onset. This chapter will discuss five methods which address trend. The first is the Tukey tri-split median-based slope, next is extended celeration or "split middle" line (ECL) (White & Haring, 1980 also seen in the literature as PEM-T; Wolery et al., 2010); and graph rotation for overlap and trend (GROT) (Parker, Vannest & Davis, 2012) then there is Tau-U for non-overlap between groups (Tau-U, Parker, Vannest, Davis, & Sauber, 2011) and Theil Sen (Vannest et al., 2012).

Median-based, hand-drawn trend lines have been used for well over a century. Early examples were given by Adcock as early as 1877, followed by Roos (1937) and a short time later Wald's (1940) seminal line-fitting article. The methods are similar; lines are drawn through medians of first and last sections of data after the series has been split into halves or thirds (Brown & Mood, 1951; Tukey, 1977). The "split middle" was popularized by White and Haring (1980), and Kazdin

(1982) in special education applications. After drawing the "split middle" trend line, it may be adjusted up or down (maintaining same slope), so half of the data-points fall above it and half below. When not adjusted, it is better known as Koenig's "quarter-intersect" method (Koenig, 1972), although it preceded Koenig by some years (Brown & Mood, 1951).

Calculated and statistical trend lines such as Tau-U and Theil-Sen are more recent but demonstrate robust effects equal to or better than linear regression without violating the assumptions of the data. These methods are most quickly calculated using software or statistics programs which are readily available for free.

Tukey Tri-split Median-Based Slope

The "Tukey" tri-split trend refers to the technique of drawing a trend line from the first to the third data segments. The method appeared in the 1940s, but was refined and popularized by Tukey and colleagues (Bartlett, 1949; Emerson & Hoaglin, 1983; Gibson & Jowett, 1957; Hoaglin, Mosteller, & Tukey, 1983; Mosteller, 1946; Tukey, 1977; Wald, 1940; Nair, & Shrivastava, 1942; Tukey, 1977). The Tukey trend line may or may not be adjusted up or down, to pass through the median of the middle data section, or to split all data 50/50, as White's "split middle" method does. Although division of data into thirds is commonly recommended, the optimal tri-part division is: 27 percent, 46 percent, 27 percent (McCabe, 1980; Stigler, 1974), giving greater influence to fewer data-points toward the ends of the trend line.

Extended Celeration Line

ECL or "split middle" line (ECL; White & Haring, 1980). ECL controls positive phase A (or baseline) trend. ECL starts with hand-fitting a bi-split median line to phase A and extending the line through phase B. The non-overlap calculation means the proportion of phase B data which are above the median slope plotted from phase A data and extended into phase B. ECL has limitations of low statistical power and ECL may not be viewed as a true non-overlap method. The comparison is the phase B datapoints overlapping an extended phase A trend line rather than directly contrasting phase A and B datapoints.

1. Using the X (horizontal) axis, find the middle data point (or space between data points) of each phase and draw a vertical line. For example a data series of 1, 2, 3, 4, 5 (or Mon, Tue, Wed, Thurs, Friday) would have "3" or "Wednesday" as the middle point. A data series of 1, 2, 3, 4, 5, 6 would have the space between 3 and 4 as the middle point (see illustration in Figures 3.11 and 3.12).

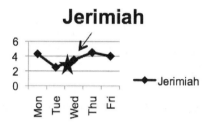

Figure 3.11 **Middle point of short data set.**

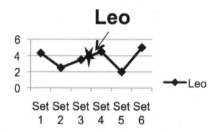

Figure 3.12 **Middle point of short data set.**

2. Find the midpoint for each of the two data sections. For example the data series 1, 2, 3, 4, 5 now has 1, 2 as one section and 4, 5 as the other section. The mid-point for each of these sections would be the space between 1 and 2 and the space between 4 and 5. (see illustration Figure 3.13)

3. Next using the Y (vertical) axis find the middle value for both sections (to the left and right of the phase middle point). For example if the range of data is from 1 to 100 the vertical middle point would be 50, if the range of the data is 1 to 5 the vertical middle would be 2.5 (see Figure 3.14).

4. For each section draw the intersection of the horizontal and vertical lines (see illustration Figure 3.15).

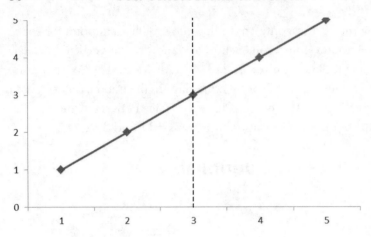

Figure 3.13 **Example of drawing a median line on the X axis.**

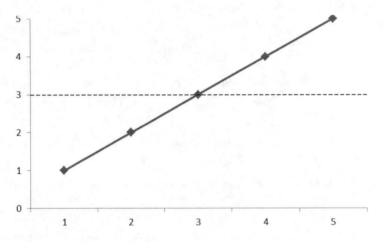

Figure 3.14 **Example of drawing a median line on the Y axis.**

5. Now draw the trend line between the intersection in section 1 and the intersection in section 2 (see illustration Figure 3.16).

Graph Rotation for Overlap and Trend

GROT (Parker, Vannest & Davis, 2012) is a hand-calculation method to control for positive baseline trend and as such it is easily accessible for use in school or clinic settings. No statistical software is needed, nor is any expertise in sophisticated methods needed. GROT is flexible for

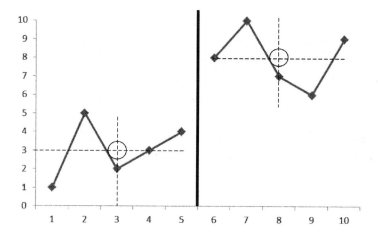

Figure 3.15 **Finding two median points in a data set.**

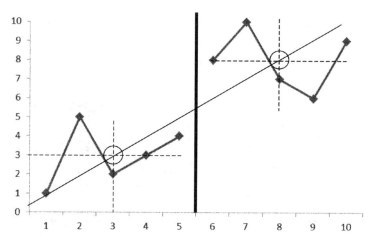

Figure 3.16 **Finding the trend line between two median points in a data set.**

any pronounced trend and allows the calculation of a non-overlap effect size. GROT offers more statistical power than ECL. ECL relies on a low power binomial test. GROT allows for a dominance or non-overlap test which has 91–94 percent of the power of a regression line. Both GROT and ECL are distribution free and robust to outliers of data. Both can be applied to ordinal and interval data or scales.

First, a trend line is hand-drawn on phase A data. Next slide or drop the trend line to the X, Y axis intersect (keeping parallel with the original line) and extended the trend line through the end point of phase B. Third, rotate the graph so that new dropped trend line becomes parallel with a new horizontal base of the graph. For example, this trend line "starts" at the Y value of about 3, the trend line would drop down to where the line becomes parallel with that value (see the arrow line in Figure 3.17).

This example data set (figure on the left) shows the trend line from phase A drawn through phase B. In the figure on the right, the graph shows a trend line rotated so as to be parallel to the X axis, the graph is then representing a "control" for the baseline and the overlap can be calculated with this adjustment. In this example NAP is used to calculate the ES.

The next example (Figure 3.18) shows the comparison between the overlap calculated before and after the rotation. Prior to an adjustment for baseline trend the ES was 99 percent, visually one can see that this

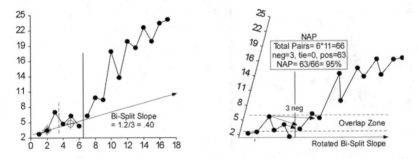

Figure 3.17 **Example of NAP calculation after bi-split trend control.**

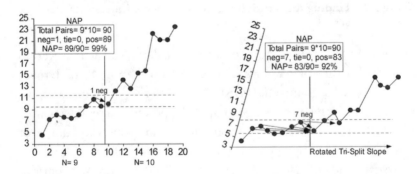

Figure 3.18 **Example of NAP calculation aftertri-split trend control.**

could be an inflated number. After GROT baseline trend is adjusted and the resulting ES of 92 percent is more comprehensible.

Notice also, that the line between the two phases (intervention onset line) is redrawn so that it is vertical and now perpendicular to the new horizontal axis. Finally, one can compare phase A and B data visually and/or statistically. We later present two statistical methods as illustrations and visual judgments as validation. The physically rotated graph has the effect of statistically controlling for phase A trend. The effect is identical to using semi-partial correlation to statistically control for baseline trend, as in the well-reputed technique by Allison, Faith and colleagues (Allison & Gorman, 1993) without the calculation.

NAP (the calculation used in this example) is a "complete" non-overlap method, as it equally considers all data points in both phases. As a complete method, it is supported by "dominance" statistics, The NAP formula is the number positives added to half (0.5) the number of ties, subtract the number of negatives and divide by the number of pairs (#Pos + 0.5 * #Ties) / #Pairs.

First, the number of data points in phase A and phase B are multiplied together to obtain the total number of paired comparisons (#Pairs). Next, the "overlap zone" is visually identified by finding the lowest phase B data point and the highest phase A data point (assuming you are expecting or desiring growth in phase B). All data in the zone is an overlap and will be counted as a "negative." Data which are identical in value are counted as a "tie." The fastest way to calculate is to count the negatives and subtract from total number of pairs to get the number of positives, this is quicker and more accurate than actually counting all the positives. A complete description of NAP is available in Parker and Vannest (2009) for interested readers.

Tau-U

Tau-U for non-overlap between groups (Tau-U; Parker, Vannest, Davis, & Sauber, 2011). Tau-U is an effect size which can account for monotonic trend. Tau U can be used at the individual phase contrast such as the techniques presented earlier, Tau U is useful in aggregating data across phases to come up with one overall or omnibus ES, and finally Tau U can be aggregated for meta-analysis. Tau U is strong, possessing statistical power of 91–115 percent of parametric tests (depending on the data) (Cliff, 1993; Delaney & Vargha, 2002; Parker, Vannest, Davis & Sauber, 2011; Wilcox, 2010) and phase A trend is controlled in a manner that is defensible for visual analyst.

Tau-U Software Application

Tau-U webpage calculation is available at: www.singlecaseresearch. org/calculators/tau-u . Data, in vertical "Time" ordered columns, can be pasted into ten data windows, one phase per window. Each phase window is labeled by the user, as, for example, "A," "A2," "B," or "C." The user then selects just two phase windows at a time to perform an individual phase contrast. Both windows are selected, and the "Contrast" button clicked. Note that Tau and Taub are provided, but the SE, Z and p-values are for the simpler Tau only. Also, some programs (for example, StatsDirect, 2008) provide superior exact p-values, rather than the approximate Z values provided by the web-page. Tau's S distribution, however, rapidly approximates the standard normal (Z) with remarkably small Ns of nine to ten (Hollander & Wolfe, 1999).

Figure 3.19 shows the web page interface for the free Tau-U Calculator and a demonstration video is also available.

Theil-Sen

Theil-Sen (Sen, 1968; Theil, 1950; Vannest et al., 2012) is a straight line fit to the data and is interpreted as rate of improvement over time, just like linear regression slope. This index is unique however in that the literal interpretation is the percent of scores which improve over time and may not be in linear fashion. This is similar to the R2 index which is interpreted as percent of score variability explained by improvement over time.

Theil-Sen is equal or superior to any other nonparametric slope estimation method in robustness and precision (Johnson & Velleman, 1985). Theil-Sen is used widely in the earth sciences (meteorology, hydrology, ecology, climatology) for high-stakes time series measurement of, for example, land erosion, glacier retreat, air and water purity, and nuclear power leakage (Hirsch & Slack 1984; Helsel & Hirsch,

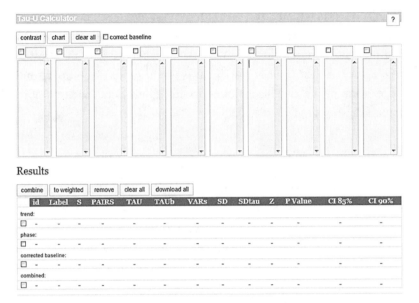

Figure 3.19 **Screen shot from www.singlecaseresearch.org.**

1992; McBride, 2000; Sheskin, 2007). It is also increasingly prominent in medical research (Helsel & Hirsch, 2002; Von Storch, 1995).

Theil-Sen software is not common, but is freely available. First, it is provided by the freely downloadable student MYSTAT 12 (SYSTAT, 2007), a junior version of SYSTAT. MYSTAT 12 offers one and two -sided confidence intervals for Theil-Sen. Theil-Sen is located under Time Series>>Slope estimator, beside Kendall's Tau. A second convenient application is OpenStat (Miller, 2010), also freely down-loadable. Theil-Sen is located under Nonparametric>>Sen's Slope. A third free source is the dedicated application, KTRLine Version 1.0, (Granato, 2006), downloadable from the US Geological Survey Office. The Theil-Sen analyses for this paper were done with StatsDirect (2008), an inexpensive program designed for medical researchers. In StatsDirect, Theil-Sen is termed "nonparametric linear regression." The above sources are menu-driven and easy to use. Less intuitive is the free open-source "R" stats program, includes Theil-Sen within its "mblm" package at: http://cran.rproject.org/web/packages/mblm/mblm.pdf. Last, for those familiar with Minitab, a macro is available: "SENSLOPE.MAC" (Akritas, 2004).

Theil-Sen is calculated by computing the slopes of all possible pairs of data-points in the time series [N*(N−1)]/2. It is conceptually straightforward but tedious to hand-calculate. So for six data points in a series or phase [6*(6−1)]/2 =15, 15 is the number of comparisons. The median value of these slopes is the Theil Sen. Each slope is calculated as =

$$\frac{Yb - Ya}{Xb - Xa}.$$

For example (Figure 3.20), in the data series for baseline data values are 6, 7, 3, 7, 8, 5, 9, 6, 7, and intervention data indicates values of 3, 2, 4, 5, 3, 1, 4, 2, 3. To calculate the slope of a phase the first step is to determine the number of comparisons. There are 9 data points in phase A Baseline and phase B Intervention. The calculation is [N*(N−1)]/2 or [9 *(9−1)]/2 or (9*8)/2 or 72/2 = 36 comparisons in either phase. Slopes are calculated by dividing each score (Y) difference by its time (X) distance. The comparisons in the intervention phase (if calculating by hand) would be 3–2, 3–4, 3–5, 3–3, 3–1, 3–4, 3–2, 3–3 (etc for all 36 comparisons) . Or 1, 1, 2, 0, 2, 1, 1, 0. The Theil-Sen slope is the median of these 36. In this selected example the median would be between the lowest value 0 and the highest value 2 so "1."

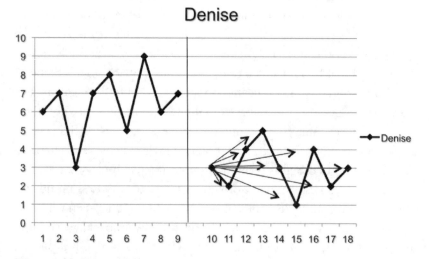

Figure 3.20 **Estimating trend in the intervention phase.**

An important thing to remember about slope is its dependency on the scale (Ardoin & Christ, 2009; Christ & Coolong-Chaffin, 2007) comparing one slope to another requires standardization. Another issue in calculating slope is the misfit of typical SCR data to the assumptions required for linear regression. Linear regression and inference testing require interval scaled data, normality of distribution, constant variance, linearity of relationship and serial independency. Progress-monitoring data or time-series data for individual students rarely meet these assumptions (Vannest et al., 2012). This is why experts promote nonparametric analysis instead (Acion, Peterson, Temple, & Arndt, 2006; D'Agostino, Campbell, & Greenhouse, 2006; Delaney & Vargha, 2002; Grissom & Kim, 2005; Wilcox, 1998), and it is also why fields like medicine (where defensibility is required and litigation is common) accept and promote robust nonparametric techniques (Armitage, Berry, & Matthews, 2002; Hollander & Wolfe, 1999). When treatment decisions are made in schools or client-service settings, the methods of analysis should likewise be resistant to legal challenge and robust in application.

There are certainly other models (besides non-overlap or dominance models) that will allow for the calculation of effect sizes in single case research, however the vast majority of data from schools does not conform to the minimum requirements needed to analyze this data. Data in SCR are typically auto correlated or possess serial dependency, the distribution of the data is unknown or non-normal, and the data itself is not of the appropriate scale. Rapid advancement in this area is being made and techniques may become available from which to utilize one or more of these powerful techniques. So this section is to inform the school psychologist of these models in general with the understanding that these techniques may not be useful for school practice at this time. Regression models, multi-level models, and randomization models are considered a more "advanced" statistical technique and may prove difficult to meld with visual analysis or have analysis which stay true to the design of the study. We express concern in using models which take the data out of the hands of the interventionist be that the school psychologist or applied behavior analyst.

There are low-stakes and high-stakes types of decisions to be made in schools. Low stakes being those which have little consequence, are not permanent, are easily reversible, and are frequently revisited. Assignment to a reading group is probably a low-stakes decision. How to assemble teams in a peer tutoring program is also probably a low-stakes decision. Conversely, high-stakes decisions are less easily reversed or may be permanent, these types of decisions may not be systematically revisited or revisited but infrequently, these types of decisions have greater consequence and thus greater weight. Analysis of single case data is useful for both purposes, but the analysis choice and the reliability of the data are more critical in high-stakes decisions.

First, single case designs are paramount for determining conclusion validity. Calculating a statistical effect size on a flawed design is nonsensical. Second, data for high-stakes decisions must have known properties of reliability via either a direct observation second observer or some estimate that the scale used is likely to be reliable, but in every case, reliability is about the score and not solely about an instrument. Finally, the more sophisticated effect size calculations may create "black-box" scenarios where a practitioner or end-user is unclear on how the data is used to calculate the ES and this may be problematic. Non parametric effect sizes such as the methods presented here are safely applied to the types of data sets commonly seen in school and clinic settings. Short time series and in conditions with less control than experimental settings.

Conclusions

Non-overlap methods for determining the effects of Single Case Research are our best recommendation for the current state-of-the-art techniques which maintain the knowledge of the interventionist in the equation. These seem best fit for school decision making and determining the evidence in a practice. They are able to be calculated by hand and can provide confidence intervals, p-values and poses reasonable levels of power. There are some weaknesses in using non-overlap, however, such as a lack of sensitivity in discriminating among the strongest and weakest effects (floor and ceiling). These techniques also have somewhat less power than other regression techniques but they require minimal assumptions about the data scale or score distribution. In any event, analysis choices should be matched to the type of data (short versus long, trended versus stable). We expect that future developments will provide new insight and possibly better methods of analysis but we should maintain the relationship between context and analysis.

4

AGGREGATION OF DATA FOR EVIDENCE-BASED PRACTICES

Practical and straightforward techniques for combining effect sizes to determine best practice. This chapter will describe combining effect sizes within a design and also across designs.

Within Single Case Research, the study design is the primary method of promoting internal validity or controlling external factors that may influence the intervention. Single Case Research often employs complex designs with multiple comparisons within a design and across dependent variables. While this complex design logic is thought to improve internal validity, aggregation of effects across a design takes special attention to unique design parameters. Consider all of the different designs in Single Case Research (such as Multiple Baseline, Reversal, Alternating Treatment, and so on). Each design provides a unique structure to control outside variables that may impact the subject's improvement or lack thereof. In turn, different designs express the effect of the intervention on the outcome variable. In order to aggregate effects within a single design and across designs, careful consideration must be given to particular design parameters, when selecting which contrasts to calculate effects sizes on.

The field of Single Case Research is currently focusing a substantial amount of attention to the issue of aggregating effect sizes within and across studies. This issue has particular importance in the ability of researchers to utilize Single Case Research in the evaluation of evidence-based practices. Current guidelines in education call for five well-designed studies to consider an intervention "evidence based."

Determining if these practices are effective individually or collectively requires the calculation of an effect size. Methods of aggregating these effects are equally important in this process.

Methods of calculating effect sizes in single case research are still widely debated. Rather than review all of these methods, the current chapter will focus on non-overlap methods to calculate effect size and the appropriate methods and decision rules to aggregate effect with these methods.

This first consideration in the process of calculating an effect size is deciding which phases to contrast. As a general rule contrasts between the baseline and the immediately adjacent intervention phase are the best choice to express the effect of an intervention with an effect size. The baseline to intervention contrast is the most authentic demonstration of intervention effect. In single case literature the baseline phase is commonly referred to as the A phase, with subsequent baselines within a design referred to with a numerical subscript. For example, a reversal design with two baselines is expressed as A1B1A2B2. Each of the baselines within this design are indicated with an A, and all of the B phases within this design represent intervention phases. Any additional intervention phases will be indicated with a new letter (usually in alphabetical order). For example, an ABCD design would have a baseline phase (that is, A), followed by three separate intervention phases (B, C, and D). Single case graphs may contain several adjacent baseline and intervention phases or just one.

Through this chapter we will explore several design modalities and how to effectively aggregate effects within many of them. This complicated process begins with the most simple of designs, the AB contrast. While an AB is not sufficient to meet internal validity standards in its own right (that is, a minimum of three phase contrasts), the AB contrast is the most basic building block that will be used to aggregate effects within and across designs. Consider a simple AB contrast (see Figure 4.1).

Effect sizes from statistical calculations tell us only the amount of client behavior change across phases. For an effect size to communicate more essential information, or show that the behavior change was due to a particular intervention, requires a strong design, visual

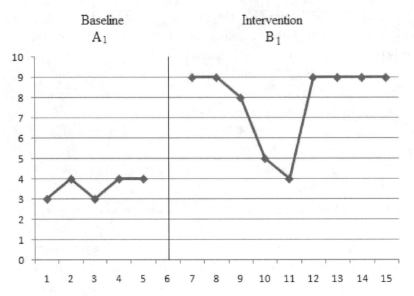

Figure 4.1 **AB design.**

analysis of response patterns (anticipated and otherwise), and strategic selection of which phases to contrast.

Regardless of the complexity of a design, statistical calculation of an effect size depends upon contrasts between phases, at the most simple level a baseline versus intervention (for example, A vs B). With multiple treatments and series, the number of possible contrasts can be very large. Only those contrasts which provide unambiguous support for a causal link between an intervention and client response should be selected. Whether a particular phase contrast can lend intuitive support to a causal inference usually requires judgment on the part of those using the data.

Given the fact that AB designs do not meet minimum standards for internal validity, users of this type of data must employ informed judgment about which intervention phases to calculate effects on. For example, given an ABCD design, the most authentic demonstration of intervention effect would be an effect size calculated on the A versus B phase. While this design does include additional interventions proto-cols within the C and D phases, one cannot determine the effect of the C or D intervention without considering "carry over" effects from the

B intervention phase. The concept of "carry over" is central to the logic of aggregating effect sizes. The primary goal of any aggregation is to consolidate many effect sizes from many studies to create a more trustworthy or robust estimate of the intervention effect. The influence of prior phases may impact the estimation of intervention effect, or the intervention conducted in the B phase may impact the improvement seen in the C phase. Consider the following example, a token economy is an intervention commonly used in schools. A token economy has many possible features that may or may not be used (for example, response cost, primary reinforcement, and so on). A study may reasonably utilize an ABC design where the A phase is baseline, the B phase is token economy with primary reinforcement, phase C is a token economy with a response cost feature. With this design, one can only calculate an authentic effect size based on the AB contrast. In this example baseline (that is, non-experimental condition) versus token economy with primary reinforcement is the only contrast that is not influenced by any other condition. To attempt to calculate an effect size based on the A versus C contrast or baseline versus token economy with response cost, one would have to consider the influence of the B phase intervention. This influence may potentially explain any or all of the gains seen in the C phase. To calculate an effect size based on A versus C would force one to concede the effect size may be influenced by factors other than the intervention procedures utilized in the C phase.

To avoid spurious results, effect size estimates should only be calculated based on adjacent phases. This will allow for an authentic estimation of intervention effect. One of the few exceptions to this rule is in the case of a training phase between baseline and intervention. A training phase can be a unique phase where the participant was exposed to experimental methods without the expectation to implement these experimental procedures. Conditions may be present that may affect participant behavior, however one would not expect a significant change in behavior given the incomplete implementation of the intervention. Some form of training is expected in any direct intervention, following non-experimental baseline conditions. Given the change in experimental conditions in the training phase, it is not logical to aggregate data from this phase with non-experimental baseline data. While excluding data is generally not advised due to intervention carry over effects mentioned above, data from a training phase represents a carry-over effect that is expected in intervention research. Therefore, the most authentic method to calculate intervention effects under these conditions is to exclude the training phase data and compare data from the non-experimental phase (baseline) to data from the experimental phase. To assure that significant change in outcome is not occurring between the baseline and training phase, a difference test between data samples (for example, Mann-Whitney U) may be used to assess differences between data in these phases. Given a non-significant difference in outcome, the change in the outcome variable can be seen as being due to the training alone.

Which Phases to Aggregate?

The question of which phases to aggregate is important, and not fully agreed upon within the scientific community. Current practice in published SCR meta-analysis is extremely variable on this topic. While some studies restrict the analysis to AB contrasts (Vannest, Davis, Davis, Mason, & Burke, 2010), others aggregate all post-baseline intervention phases into a single data stream (Preston & Carter, 2009). Given differences in intervention protocol between phases, the aggregation of intervention phases requires careful consideration. The identity of the outcome summary will likely suffer if the phase contrast aggregation is not carefully considered. Furthermore, one must consider if the effects are dependent (correlated) or independent (uncorrelated). Most effect sizes calculated from within a single design should be considered uncorrelated or independent, although full independence from a single organism is difficult to argue. The best argument for independence of effects is the intent and logic built into the design, that is, most phase shifts are assumed independent, and score patterns should be examined to confirm that assumption.

While this logic may work for independent effects, dependent effects require additional considerations. Recommended aggregation methods for combining dependent or correlated effect sizes are different from that described above, and yield much more conservative results (Hedges

& Olkin, 1985). If the effect sizes are considered to be correlated, then combining effects across contrasts would offer little or no advantage, for example, a multiple baseline design with six tiers would offer about the same precision as a single AB contrast. Issues of correlation quickly become apparent, however, when one attempts to calculate multiple effect sizes on a single phase. For example, in an ABA reversal design (see Figure 4.2), the two contrasts A1 vs B and B vs A2 are clearly dependent, that is, the results from the first A1 vs B contrast constrain results attainable from B vs A1. Thus, effects from two contrasts, which share a phase, may be considered dependent. Given these considerations, the effect sizes should not calculated based on contrasts with shared phases.

An added intervention component without a legitimate return to baseline, cannot be reasonably attributed to the intervention components used in that phase. Therefore "carry over" effects may impact the measurement of improvement. This is of particular importance in aggregation, where intervention procedures may vary. Consider again the token economy example above. If the ABC design was changed to an ABAC design, a legitimate return to baseline would reasonably cleanse the data of the influence of the intervention implemented in

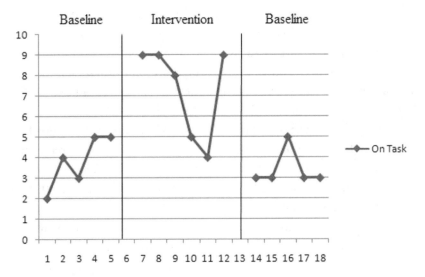

Figure 4.2 **ABA design.**

the B phase. A legitimate return to baseline occurs when the data return to a level seen in the original baseline. This shows that the intervention effects have not generalized to the study participant, or the intervention is no longer impacting the participant's behavior. Given a return to baseline, one could reasonably calculate two separate effect sizes from this design. In the ABAC example, an authentic effect can reasonably be calculated on the A versus B and A versus C contrasts separately. Aggregation of the effect sizes should be done with careful consideration of desired outcome, however. Within the Token economy example an aggregation of AB with AC would create a single effect size for a token economy with primary reinforcers and token economy with response cost. If the goal of this aggregation is to make a summary statement about token economy with a variety of added components than this would be appropriate. If, however, the goal is to make a statement regarding the effectiveness of token economy with response cost only then aggregation would not be permitted. The decision regarding which effect sizes to aggregate is of particular importance to the conclusions or inferences you can draw from these results. It is important to use judgment to ensure that the effect sizes being aggregated match in experimental features, or simply that the interventions being compared are the same.

In order to aggregate effects, two essential pieces of information must be calculated. First the effect size, and second the variance. The effect size is the standardize measure of improvement or non-improvement. The variance is how far apart the scores are from one another, or how much spread there is in the data. For example, see Figure 4.3. Figure 4.3 has very little variance, the scores are fairly consistent and only range between four and five on the y-axis. In contrast, Figure 4.4 has a very high variance, you can see the scores are very spread out across the y-axis and a range from one to ten.

The variance is a necessary ingredient in aggregating the effect size for several reasons. First the variance is an estimate of how trustworthy any point estimate is from a given data set. For example, look at the mean for Figures 4.3 and 4.4. Figure 4.3 has a mean of 3.6. This point is very close to all other points in the data set. This is because the data points do not vary much from one another.

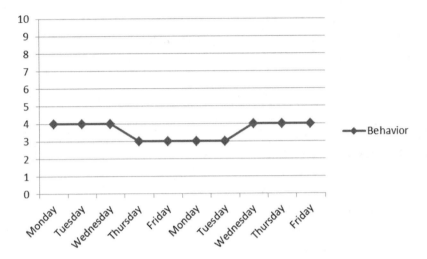

Figure 4.3 **Stable data.**

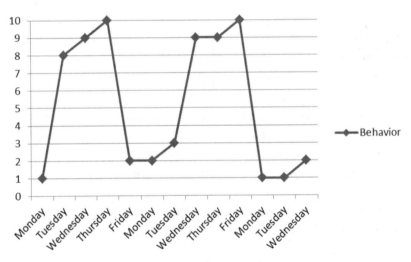

Figure 4.4 **Highly variable data.**

The variance for the data in Figure 4.3 is 0.24, and can be interpreted as the average squared deviation from the mean across the population of data points that the sample represents. In contrast Figure 4.4 has a mean of 5.15 which a less accurate summary of the data available in this graph. The variance score of 1.99 reflects the large amount of spread in the data in Figure 4.4. Although the previous example discusses means, the variance around any point estimate (including effect sizes) gives an index of certainty one can have in the summary estimate of the data. Therefore, the variance is an important consideration in aggregating effect sizes.

Specifically, the variance is used as the preferred method to control the influence of an effect size when aggregating among other effect sizes. This is because an effect size that is calculated from data with high variability is less trustworthy than a similar effect size that is calculated from data with low variability. To control this, effect sizes should be weighted. The most accepted method for combining effect size is to weight each effect size by the inverse of the variance and divide this value by the sum of the weights (Hedges & Olkin, 1985; Shadish & Haddock, 1994).

Methods to aggregate effect sizes have been a particular concern in single case research due to the fact that data sets often have such small amounts of data. Accepted benchmarks for the amount of data in a phase are three points. With such few data points it is necessary to use effect size metrics that are appropriate. Many effect sizes require that certain assumptions be met by the data. For full review of effect sizes see Chapter 3.

The Tau-U effect size is particularly innovative due to the fact that it is appropriate for short data series typical in single case research and multiple phase contrasts can be easily aggregated. Tau-U uses the S distribution, to determine the variance score (Vars). Tau-U effects can be averaged after weighting each effect size by the inverse of the variance score (Vars). Furthermore, Tau-U standard errors can be aggregated by the following methods: 1.) Squaring individual standard error scores, 2.) Summing these squares, and 3.) Taking the square root of the sum. This method of aggregation has long been recommended for group design meta-analysis (Hedges & Olkin, 1985).

Multiple Base Line Design

One of the more common designs in single case research is the multiple baseline design. This design has the benefit of concurrent control of external variables that may affect the validity of the outcome. Consider a multiple base line design with three subjects (see Figure 4.5).

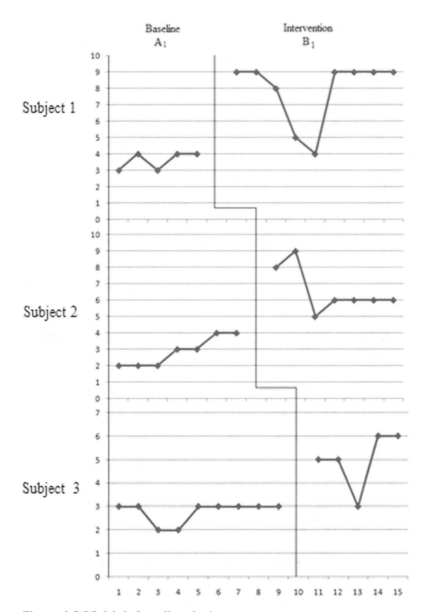

Figure 4.5 **Multiple baseline design.**

A strong MBD design includes three series with AB, each of the three intervention onset points and concurrent baseline controls for comparison A visual inspection of this graph shows expected improvement in all three AB patterns, and no evidence of the confounding

　　　　　　　　AGGREGATION DATA

Table 4.1 **Data for the Figure 4.5**

	Tau U	Variance	Reciprocal of the Variance (i.e. Weight)
Student 1	0.9333	225	0.004444
Student 2	1	245	0.004082
Student 3	0.8444	225	0.004444
Total	0.9281		

influence of external events in the concurrent control phases. Therefore, our design and data patterns permit calculation of an effect size for each of the three AB contrasts. Given that our design meets criteria for internal validity, we may then proceed to calculating three separate effect sizes and may also combine these separate effect sizes to calculate an aggregate design-wide effect size.

The analysis is of those phase contrasts are essential to the logic of the MBD design. Therefore, the contrasts contributing to an omnibus MBD omnibus effect are:

• Student 1: A vs B
• Student 2: A vs B
• Student 3: A vs B

Combination of individual effect size occurs after they are weighted by the inverse of their variance. This has the effect of giving more weight to results which come from a larger number of data points and which show less variability.

ABABA Reversal Design

Another commonly used design within single case research is the reversal design (see Figure 4.6). The data in this example show a consistent effect across phases, a legitimate return to baseline, although separation of data between phases is less than ideal.

In order to trust effect sizes as indicators of intervention effectiveness, their calculation should be preceded with a visual check for a) data patterns, which suggest alternative causes of improvement or

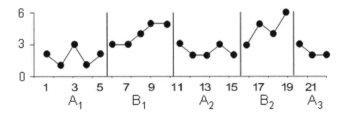

Figure 4.6 **Reversal design.**

lack of improvement, and b) consistent results across all key phase contrasts. Neither of those concerns are evident in the graph, so effect size calculation continues.

The first step in the analysis of this data is consideration of which phases to contrast. For this example, we have A1, B1, A2, B2, and A3. Data for each of the five phases may be appropriate for further analysis given the fact that visual inspection has indicated that the overall design meets standards for internal validity. The most intuitive contrast would be A1 vs B1 and by A2 vs B2 since these are adjacent phases. The final phase A3 is not followed by an intervention phase so this facet of the design will most likely be left out of further analysis. One could analyze B2 vs A3, but this analysis raises two significant problems. First, if A1 vs B1 is to be analyzed, the intended direction of the intervention is the opposite of B2 vs A3. More simply put, A1 vs B1 represents improvement through the addition of an intervention, and B2 vs A3 represents regression through withdrawal of the intervention. Second, if aggregated, the effect of the intervention would be nullified due to the fact that intended improvement and non-improvement are aggregated together. Third, an attempt to include B2 vs A3 in a formula would exclude inclusion of A2. Since A2 and A3 share an adjacent baseline these contrasts would be considered correlated, given the shared phase B2. Given these issues, the most intuitive single contrasts for this graph are A1 vs B1 and A2 vs B2. Calculation with the Tau U effect size would yield the data in Table 4.2

Table 4.2 Data for Figure 4.7

	Tau U	Variance	Reciprocal of the Variance (i.e. Weight)
A1 vs B1	0.92	91.6667	0.010909
A2 vs B2	0.90	66.6667	0.015
Total	0.9106		

Comparing Effects Across Designs

Aggregating study effects across designs follows similar logic to aggregating effect sizes within a design, but this process is much easier due to the fact that selecting which contrasts to aggregate is already taken care of in the within design calculation. Mathematically, the process is identical to the within design process of aggregating effects. The two primary ingredients still are necessary, effect size and the variance from that effect size. Each study effect size will be weighted by the inverse of the variance then summed together and divided by the sum of the weights. See Figure 4.7 below for mathematical formula in question.

This formula only demonstrates the aggregation of two studies. Additional studies can be aggregated simply by adding the weighted the effect size in the numerator and the accompanying weight in the denominator.

- *Comparing Effects*   Many times there are variables of interest that one may want to analyze from a particular set of studies. For example one may want to determine if males or females respond better to a particular intervention. Analysis of these variables can follow standard practice for analyzing categorical variables (Agresti, 1996; Siegel & Castellan, 1988). These variables can be coded separately (for example, gender, age, etc), and then sets of effect sizes from

$$\frac{\left((\textit{Effect size Study 1}) * \frac{1}{\textit{variance Study 1}}\right) + \left((\textit{Effect size Study 2}) * \frac{1}{\textit{variance Study 2}}\right)}{\frac{1}{\textit{variance Study 1}} + \frac{1}{\textit{variance Study 2}}}$$

Figure 4.7 **Formula for weighting effect sizes.**

studies that contain that particular variable can be compared to determine statistically significant differences. Two variables comparisons (for example, male and female) can be evaluated using the Mann-Whitney U statistic. Three variable comparisons (for example, elementary, middle school, and high school) can be evaluated with the Kruskal-Wallis one-way analysis of variance. Both of these analytic techniques can be found in most commercially available statistical packages.

5

BEHAVIORS OF INTEREST
AND THEIR RELIABLE
MEASUREMENT

Broadening the permissible "target behaviors" from traditional ABA to a broader array of reliably measured outcomes increases the applicability of single case research to a variety of behavior rating scales such as those seen in daily behavior report cards. This data is then useful in determining responsiveness to intervention and in making decisions about school or clinic programming. Estimation scales, qualitative ratings as well as frequency counts are all viable measures for behaviors of interest. This practical discussion and demonstration addresses the range of options available.

Measurement is the process of determining the amount or quantity of a desired construct. In education, we desire to measure student behaviors or academic skills. The current emphasis on measurement of student progress in Response to Intervention (RTI) models makes the process of accurate measurement increasingly important. Proper measurement is the foundation by which educators determine a student's level of skill and progress. Despite the obvious importance of accurate measurement, this process is rarely approached with the level of conceptual rigor necessary to assure that the desired construct is appropriately assessed. The chapter outlines three basic guidelines that should serve as a guide in measurement. First, determine the purpose of the measurement. Second, build these constructs. Third, construct items that best assess the desired student behavior or skill. A detailed conceptual model is provided for each of these three guidelines and examples provide a framework to approach the practice of measurement.

The process of measurement involves procedures in which student behaviors or skills are obtained, scored, and evaluated using standardized procedures (AERA, APA, NCME, 1999). Due to the fact that a test is only a sample of behavior or skills, it is imperative that the measure reflect a representative sample of behavior or skills that are of interest (Crocker & Algina, 2006). The score that is produced by our measurement is a summary of the evidence contained in an examinee's responses or behaviors that are related to the construct or constructs being measured (Reynolds, Livingston, & Willson, 2006). The scores that are produced are the foundation of judgments made about a person's behavior or skill in a particular domain. Statistical estimates (for example, effect sizes) depend largely on the planning and preparation before the measurement device is created. This process will help to assure that the measurement device created will assess the desired construct and produce scores that are descriptive of a person's skill or behavior.

Guideline 1: Determine the Purpose of the Measurement

The development of any measurement device should begin with consideration of how and for whom the scores will be used (Crocker & Algina, 2006). These scores may be used in a variety of applications such as making eligibility decisions, placement, or for diagnostic purposes. A single measurement will be unlikely to meet the needs of each of these separate areas.

When the purpose of the test is to compare an individual with the performance of others on a particular construct, this is a norm-reference test. Psychological constructs such as intelligence and academic functioning are commonly assessed in this manner. This is because the degree to which individuals differ in the amount of an attribute, or differ from the norm is of primary interest (Crocker & Algina, 2006). In norm-referenced test interpretation, scores are compared with an appropriate norm group. This is done by comparing various demographic characteristics of the individuals making up the test group and the norm group to ensure their similarity (Reynolds, Livingston, & Willson, 2006).

An alternative to a norm referenced test is a criterion-referenced test. A criterion test score is not compared to other examinees, but is judged in terms of the examinee's absolute level of proficiency. This type of assessment is generally associated with teacher-made achievement testing and behavioral assessment (Reynolds, Livingston, & Willson, 2006).

Guideline 2: Building the Constructs

Building an understanding of the construct to be measured requires preparation and considerable due diligence on the part of the test creator. Reliance on intuition alone may result in biased or flawed models of the construct. Crocker & Algina (2006) suggest the following activities to build a better understanding of the construct to be assessed. First, elicit information from the individuals that have regular interaction with the student (for example, parents and teachers), as well as the student themself. When interviewing these individuals, consider open ended questions to gain information about the construct of interest. These responses can then be sorted into topical categories, and the topics that occur most frequently are used as major components of the construct. This will help to organize your process and may help illuminate priorities for measurement. Creating constructs about behaviors is useful in progress monitoring where a normed instrument is unavailable or prohibited. Some states and districts lack resources for purchasing commercially available instruments. Some states and districts have philosophical or legal reasons for preferring locally created measures. It is common to see professionals move from a well-constructed and established instrument to a direct observation approach of frequency counts, duration or latency of operationally defined behavior. However, topographical and categorical descriptions of behavior can produce reliable results which are more efficient for data collection in instructional or home settings, and capture a number of discrete behaviors at one time.

Creating the Measurement Tool

Often measurement creators will conceptualize one or more types of behavior which are believed to manifest a particular construct and then simply "think up" items that demonstrate the desired behaviors (Crocker

& Algina, 2006). For example, depression scales developed before the 1980s (for example, Hamilton rating scale for depression (Ham-D), Montgomery-Asberg Depression Rating Scale (MADRS), and the Young Mania Rating Scale (YMRS) tended to overemphasize symptoms of endogenous depression, and did not include items pertaining to atypical symptoms such as hyperphagia and hypersomnia. This overemphasis was believed to significantly under-identify subpopulations of individuals with depression (Rush, First, & Blacker, 2008).

In addition to identifying constructs and subsequent items such as those commonly found in test development, behaviors may be identified based on their social importance in a classroom or clinic setting. These behaviors may be identified because they are a problem to decrease or because they are a goal behavior to increase. Behavior or skill goals are social expectations that are observable, measureable, and meaningful to teachers and students. Behavior targets should be observable and quantifiable. Observable behaviors do not include feelings or intentions which are inferred from other behaviors. Observable and measurable targets allow campus staff to document growth or change in student behavior. Meaningful goals are sensitive to the culture and behavioral expectations in the classroom. When written effectively, individual behavior goals can create a positive learning environment.

Clearly defined behavioral goals improve each teacher's ease and accuracy of documenting the occurrence or non-occurrence of the expected behavior. When teachers agree on the same behavioral constructs, communication between teachers and parents or teacher and teacher improves. Creating constructs by identifying target behaviors allows for a standardized method of measurements across teachers and staff for combining or contrasting student performance.

In addition to aiding measurement, clearly identified individual behavior or skill goals provides teachers, parents, and students with the following benefits:

1. A common set of expectations
2. A language for communication between teachers and students/ parents
3. Guidance for existing behavior/skill expectations
4. Teaching opportunities

Guideline 3: Construct Scales That Best Assess the Desired Construct

How to Identify Behaviors / Skills

After identifying or recognising the audience of the measurement, and identifying constructs, the final step is to identify the behaviors and skills specifically to be measured. The first step to progress monitoring is identifying student behaviors or skills that need improvement. When selecting student behaviors to monitor, stakeholders at the school should consider monitoring Individual Education Plan (IEP) goals or Behavior Improvement Plan (BIP) goals, for students already receiving special education services. For students not in special education, one may consider behaviors that the teachers identify as problematic, for example skills that do not meet age or grade level expectations. School-wide expectations may also be monitored or items indicated on a risk assessment could be targeted.

Sources for Goals

Since the goal of progress monitoring is to monitor student progress, gain information for intervention planning purposes, and evaluate student performance in comparison to norms or criterion, it is best to monitor behaviors that provide stakeholders with the most relevant information. First, consider possible sources for identification of problem behavior.

1. *IEP or BIP goals*   By monitoring IEP or BIP goals, a teacher will be ready to show evidence of a student's progress towards goals at group decision-making meetings. By utilizing this information, stakeholders make informed decisions about further goals and interventions.
2. *Teacher selected behaviors*   Sometimes, teachers have behavior concerns not addressed by the student's IEP or BIP goals. In this case, it may be most useful to select behaviors that the teacher feels are most important to the student's education. This may include behaviors that violate classroom rules or that result in office referrals. For example, "disrespect." Disrespect could be scaled and

monitored by level or type of disrespectful behavior. Eye rolling for example would be very minor compared to verbal refusal and confrontation in class.

3. *Parent behavior concerns* Integrating parent concerns with goals identified at school helps to connect home and school in the common goal of improving the student's behavior. For example, "John starts to follow directions but never finishes the task and I find him doing something else." This could be revised as a progress monitoring item of "task incompletion."

4. *School-wide expectations* These behaviors have been identified by school personnel or school leadership as reflecting the values of the school and serve as indicators of successful performance in school. For example "preparedness" might be scaled as a 1–5 or an ABCDF grade.

5. *Items which identify risk on a risk assessment* Individual items from one or more risk screeners which are identifying elevated or clinically elevate levels of risk may be appropriate to monitor as well. For example, "cries frequently" might be monitored as number of crying events daily or percentage of time the child is crying or demonstrating sad behaviors.

Steps for Selecting Behaviors

After identifying possible behaviors, evaluate the behaviors to see if the behaviors allow for easy, reliable progress monitoring. It may take work to identify the optimal number of goals to monitor. In addition, some rules may require rewording in order to maximize ease of use for progress monitoring.

1. *Number of behaviors* Typically, 3–5 behavioral indicators sum up the student's most problematic behaviors. Monitoring more than 3–5 behaviors is time consuming and burdensome and probably would not be successfully intervened with in any event so choose a workable number. Taking data for data's sake is not productive.

2. *Positive phrasing* Since we are working towards a "goal" behavior, positively phrase each behavior. Positively phrased behaviors are behaviors that the teachers want the student to ultimately exhibit.

3. *Specificity*   Explain the behavior or skill in enough detail that an independent observer could identify an occurrence or non-occurrence of a behavior. The specificity of this description will help improve communication between the teacher and other stake-holders.

Considerations

When multiple individuals will be using the scale, it is helpful if all individuals can choose and evaluate behaviors as a team. Since the student may exhibit different behavior across settings, a group effort will be more likely to address the student's full range of behavior.

Scale Construction

Several formats are available for scale, generally one must consider the content and desired test use when choosing scale format. The following section discusses a variety of scale formats with construction guideline for each.

Simple Occurrence/Non-Occurrence Scales

An occurrence/non-occurrence scale is simply a judgment of yes or no, did the event occur during a specified period? These types of scales are good for easily defined events or episodes (for example, bed-wetting, fist fights, purging, etc.). These types of scales are also good when all episodes are very similar (that is, vary little in quality and degree). While these types of scales are good for many purposes, their primary shortcoming is that they do not show the graduation necessary to monitor progress effectively for behaviors or skills. For example if the goal is to monitor student anger, a "yes/no" scale can determine if the student shows some base level of anger, however, information will be lost regarding the qualitative aspects of that child's anger. As we know there is a difference between a student who may show anger by balling their fist and one who physically attacks a police officer. This degree of anger will likely be lost in a scale that only has two categories. Scenarios are provided below with detailed examples of occurrence/non-occurrence type behaviors.

SCENARIO 1: HOMEWORK COMPLETION

Dalton's teacher is interested in participation in homework. His teacher is only interested in having the students attempt the entire homework assignment, since questions missed will be the subject of the instruction for that period. An occurrence/non-occurrence scale that captures Dalton's homework completion would be a simple yes or no scale which could be completed by the student or the teacher.

CIRCLE ONE: Did Dalton complete his homework?   YES   NO

SCENARIO 2: HAIR PULLING

Ms. Wimberly is interested in documenting one of her students' antisocial behaviors in her junior high Language Arts classroom. Her student, Jimmy is a bright and capable student with a diagnosis of obsessive compulsive disorder. This student has worked hard to control his compulsive hair pulling behavior and rarely exhibits this behavior in class. Anecdotal reports from Ms. Wimberly show that this behavior is largely under control, but may occur once or twice a week. With such a low frequency behavior, a simple occurrence/non-occurrence scale would be appropriate to document the behavior across each period of the week.

CHECK ONE: Did Jimmy engage in hair-pulling behavior?   YES   NO

Likert Items

Likert items are commonly used in the assessment of behavior or attitudes. A Likert item consists of two parts: a stem, which is simply a statement of an attitude, and a scale on which the examinee can express their agreement with that statement. A single Likert item rarely provides useful information simply because responses to it are affected by many factors in addition to the one you're interested in.

When several items are used, the consistency of responding produced by an attitude can be detected. To accomplish this task, Likert items are scaled. For example, values may be assigned to each point on the scale. For example, *Disagree strongly* could be assigned the value one, *Disagree somewhat* could be assigned two, and so on. A reliability analysis would then be performed. For the reliability analysis you would calculate a reliability coefficient (a measure of the similarity between items) and the correlations of each item with the total score. Items which did not correlate would be omitted from the scale and the reliability analysis performed again. Further refinements can increase the scale's discriminatory power. When several items are used, the consistency of responding produced by an attitude can be detected (Guilford, 1954).

The analysis of Likert items has created a controversy regarding the level of measurement that can be used in analysis. Many regard such items as ordinal data because one cannot assume that all adjacent levels of the scale are equidistant. Others contend interval level measurement is permissible due to the fact that the wording of response levels clearly implies symmetry of response levels about a middle category. The authors are of the opinion that Likert items should be viewed as ordinal scaled variables and should be analyzed as such. Clearly there are special exceptions to this rule; however the common practice of applying parametric analysis techniques to ordinal scales is better avoided.

Likert items are a very versatile type of scale that can be further classified by the construction of the scale indicators. Scale indicators are the descriptions of each point in the scale. For example, a five point scale would have five indicators with five discreet descriptions of each point.

How to Construct a Scale

- *What is Scaling?*   A scale is an ordered set of judgments that define levels of behavior quality, with numbers attached to each level. Scaling is the process of isolating behavior into component parts that show levels of progress toward a behavioral goal. Scaling is a method to convey skill attainment and skill fluency explicitly. As a student makes progress toward a behavioral goal, educators can document the attainment of skills.

- *Why do we need to scale goals?* Scaling behavior enables educators to structure their observations in ways that can be consistently communicated to the student, other educators, and families. In addition, change over time in relevant behaviors can be tracked and communicated. Scaling behavior through a collaborative process, creates continuity among educators, and establishes a common language for discussing student behavior. A common issue that confronts educators in meetings regarding student discipline is consensus on the content and severity of the behavior in question. When a student behavior has occurred over time with varying degrees of severity, discussion of the behavior is often complicated by the teacher's memory and proximity to the student's behavior incidents. By creating behavior scales before consequences are discussed, educators can be assured that the student behavior profile is accurately portrayed in terms of behavioral events and severity.

Scales can be constructed with many different numbers of points. Common scales used in education have between three and ten scale points. A consideration when deciding how many points to put on your scale is the level of sensitivity to change you need in order to show progress. As the number of points on the scale increases, the sensitivity to change also increases. The downside to having scales with larger numbers of indicators is that these scales are more difficult to obtain reliability on. As a general rule we recommend using scales with five or seven indicators. Some general guidelines to consider when constructing a five point scale are as follows. Each scale indicator can be labeled with a letter grade: A, B, C, D or F or with numbers 1–7. Given that a student has been identified as having behavior problems or skill deficit, typical current performance is described at the lower end of the scale or the "D" category in an A–F scale. This is because we are typically interested in using the scale to show progress rather than regression. So the more points you have to show progress, the more sensitivity your scale will give you toward that goal. The description for category "F" should be low enough to capture the student on a "bad day." Category "C" should describe some improve-ment above current behavior. Category "B" should describe good progress beyond current behavior toward meeting a long-term behavioral goal. Category "A" should describe behavior which is acceptable given school and class norms, and which reflects attain-ment of a long-term behavioral goal. Specific steps for scaling are as follows.

1. Identify a range of performance. Create an observable description of the behavior at its worst, which will be the floor of the scale. For example, an "F" on a five point scale. Then create an observable description of the desired behavior, this will be the ceiling of the scale or an "A" on a five point scale.
2. Designate the current behavior as an anchor. Create an observable description of the typical exhibited behavior. Place this behavior in the lower 25 percent of the scale. For example, a "D" on a five point scale. This placement on the scale will allow for the display of growth. Then, create the "B" and "C" points on the scale using observable descriptions of target behaviors that would constitute movement from the current behavior to desired behavior.
3. Check for scale validity with stakeholders. Review the created scales with key stakeholders such as teachers, co-teachers, administrators, counselors, parents, and students. Modify behavioral descriptions that are unclear.

• *Considerations*   Scaling behaviors is often less intuitive than one thinks. It takes time to create descriptions of behavior that are easily observable. Often, creating these descriptions will be a process with adjustments along the way. Using multiple informants will create the validity of created scales. Examples of several methods by which to construct a scale are provided below.

Frequency scales

A frequency scale is constructed as the number or count of responses per unit of time. Target behaviors are defined, observed, and counted or "tallied" within specified observation windows. The positive features of this type of scale include high reliability of coding and flexibility. The observation window can be further delimited, (for example, while teacher is at front of room) to produce a more specific observation period (for example, talk-outs per minute while teacher is at front of room). This can be summarized as "rate per time unit" or as "behavior comparison" (for example, "ratio per opportunity"). These types of scales do have limiting features, however. First, validity—the most easily coded events often capture only part of a needs area. Second, frequency scales may be inadequate if the coded events vary greatly in quality. Third, these scales assume equal opportunities for events to occur for all observation periods.

Further examples of frequency scales can be seen below with scenarios designed to mimic common situations where frequency scales may be used.

Scenario 1: Maintaining "On-task" Behavior

Mr. Shell thinks Maria could achieve more, but she is always off task. Mr. Shell estimates that Maria spends about 20 percent of her time on task in an average day. Mr. Shell considers "on task" to mean following activity directions within 30 seconds of being asked with no longer than 30 second breaks from the task.

• *Scaling* It will be easy for Mr. Shell to record the approximate percent of time Maria spends on task during each subject period (see Table 5.1). Also, recording the percent of time Maria is on task

Table 5.1 **Example five-point scale for On-Task behavior**

Behavior	Indicator				
	A	B	C	D	F
On-task: Will follow activity directions within 30 seconds of being asked with no longer than 30 second breaks from the task	On-task 90% of class time	On task 70% of class time	On task 50% of class time	On-task 20% of class time	On-task less than 20% of class time

by subject will allow Mr. Shell to see which classes and times of the day Maria is more likely to be on task.

SCENARIO 2: INAPPROPRIATE VERBAL INTERACTIONS

Mrs. Bright and Mr. Sunny are frustrated with John's verbal interruptions in their classes. Mrs. Bright calls a meeting of all of John's teachers to develop a behavior scale. At the meeting, all teachers agreed that John sometimes talks to peers in the middle of lectures, which disrupts their classes. Usually, he talks a moderate amount throughout class, disrupting a small group.

- *Scaling*   Since teachers are concerned with both the frequency and severity of John's talking behavior, a scale that describes the different types of behavior John exhibits in order of frequency and severity will best show growth (Table 5.2).

SCENARIO 3: INAPPROPRIATE PHYSICAL INTERACTIONS

Mrs. Smith wants "being nice" to be one of Tommy's behavior goals. Specifically, she is concerned that Tommy hits, bites and scratches his classmates around four times a day.

Table 5.2 **Example five-point scale for appropriate verbal interactions**

Behavior	Indicator				
	A	*B*	*C*	*D*	*F*
Verbal interactions: Will only talk during lectures when instructed by the teacher	Talks only when called upon by a teacher	Talks once without being called upon, disrupting only one peer	Talks 2 to three times without being called upon, disrupting a small group of peers	Talks 4 to 5 times without being called upon, disrupting a small group of peers	Talks more than 6 times without being called upon, disrupting whole class or smaller peer groups

Table 5.3 **Example five-point scale for aggressive behavior**

Behavior	Indicator				
	A	B	C	D	F
Physical interactions: Maintain appropriate physical interactions with peers	No incidents of hitting, biting or scratching peers	One incident of hitting, biting or scratching a peer	Two to three incidents of hitting, biting or scratching a peer	Four incidents of hitting, biting or scratching a peer	More than four incidents of hitting, biting or scratching a peer

- *Scaling* Since Tommy's behavior only occurs a few times a day, it may be easiest to count the number of times Tommy's behavior occurs in a day (Table 5.3).

Duration Scales

A duration scale is similar to a frequency scale, however, this type of scale documents the amount of time behavior or skill occurs. The duration scale has the same positive and negative features as the frequency scale, and should be used in situations where the increase or reduction of a certain behavior is the goal. Specific scales and scenarios are provided below.

SCENARIO 1: ON TASK

Ms. Grote needs her class to remain on task for the majority of the 60-minute period. Given transition activity at the beginning and end of the period, she would like to see her students actively on task for at least 50 minutes. She has targeted three students for whom she would like to document progress. She will use the five point scale shown in Table 5.4.

SCENARIO 2: STAYING IN SEAT

Ms. Maxey has a student Bre who is having trouble staying in her seat or designated area during group work. Ms. Maxey is interested in the total amount of time she leaves her seat to go and sharpen her pencil, talk to other students at their desks, and so on. Although there may be

Table 5.4 **Example five-point scale for on-task behavior**

Behavior	Indicators				
	A	B	C	D	F
The student will remain on task for the duration of the assignment	60–50 minutes	49–30 minutes	29–15 minutes	14–5 minutes	Less than 5 minutes

Table 5.5 **Example five–point scale for staying in assigned area**

Behavior	Indicators				
	A	B	C	D	F
The student will stay in assigned seat or designated area	Student stays in designated area for the entire class	Student leaves area for 15–30 seconds	Student leaves area for 30–60 seconds	Student leaves area for 60–90 seconds	Student leaves area for 90+ seconds

other facets to this behavior, at this time Ms. Maxey is only interested in documenting the time spent off task (see Table 5.5).

SCENARIO 3: SCREAMING

Mr. Judy is a teacher in a classroom that serves students with severe and profound disabilities. One of his students, Lacy, compulsively screams during class. Sometimes this screaming behavior goes on for more than 45 minutes. Mr. Judy is interested in reducing this behavior, and prior to initiating a functional behavior analysis, the school psychologist requested that he document the duration of screaming behavior in each class period to determine if there are any trends in this behavior over the day. To accomplish this goal, Mr. Judy constructs a scale (see Table 5.6).

Table 5.6 **Example five–point scale for inappropriate voice volume**

Behavior	Indicators				
	A	B	C	D	F
The student uses appropriate voice volume in the classroom	Student does not scream in class	Student screams for 10 or fewer minutes	Student screams for 11 to 30 minutes	Student screams for 31 to 45 minutes	Student screams for more than 45 minutes

Qualitative Judgment Scales

The final type of Likert scale discussed in this chapter is the qualitative judgment scale. This type of scale differs from the frequency and duration scales in that the scale indicators describe qualities of the behavior or skill rather than discreet instances or amount of time a behavior is elicited. This type of scale paints a "holistic" picture of complex constellations of behavior which can be readily recognized in real life. This type of scale requires specific descriptions of the scale indicators. These descriptions need not be parallel from one category to the next.

Some positive features of this type of scale include:

1. intuitive appeal, especially if the rater "knows" the student
2. quick and simple to use; to code an event, a single decision is made
3. useful for complex behavior constellations; maintains focus on the "big picture," and
4. often has high face validity and content validity.

Some potential negative features of this type of scale are:

1. usefulness of scale depends upon the cohesiveness of all indicator description *(they must occur together)*
2. reliable coding may be influenced by the raters familiarity with the student.

Specific scales and scenarios detailing potential uses are below:

SCENARIO 1: ACCEPTING REDIRECTION

Mr. Vann is a behavior coach, he consults with several behavior units across many districts. He has recommended an intervention for a student and is interested to see the student's progress in his absence. Mr. Vann and the teacher construct the following scale to document a student's explosively aggressive behavior when redirected by the teacher. After several observations, Mr. Vann has determined common observable behaviors occur, that indicate the severity of the students behavior. In order to capture this student's behavior progress based on common indicators he has seen, Mr. Vann constructs the scale shown in Table 5.7.

SCENARIO 2: LYING

Mrs. Styer has a first-grade student who is very contentious and seems overly concerned with others' approval of her. Mrs. Styer has noticed that this student will often lie if she does not think that others will like her or approve of what she is doing. Mrs. Styer has also noticed that this student is very protective of her ego and will not admit if she has told a lie. Mrs. Styer is interested in documenting this lying behavior and the student's ability to admit her lie when confronted. Based on a

Table 5.7 **Example five–point scale for accepting redirection**

Behavior	Indicators				
	A	B	C	D	F
The student will accept adult redirection without complaint	Reacts to redirection without argument	Controlled argument without cursing or putting others down	Controlled argument, with cursing, hitting desk, kicking desk, causes a distraction in immediate area; doesn't stop classroom from functioning	Arguing with requests for redirection by yelling, cursing and creating a classroom distraction; stops the classroom from functioning	Outwardly aggressive behavior, may be physically aggressive to others, or destructive to school property

progression of behaviors toward the goal of telling the truth, Ms. Styer constructs the scale shown in Table 5.8.

SCENARIO 3: FIGHTING

Ms. Chavez is the assistant principal at a large High School. One of her "Frequent Flyers" Julio continues to get referrals to the office for fighting. Ms. Chavez has worked with Julio for several years and knows his behavior well. Ms. Chavez only sees Julio when he is in trouble and would like to facilitate a more positive relationship with him. She has asked his teachers to record his behavior so that she can "catch him being good," in addition she is interested to see how many times he initiates aggressive acts that may not require a referral to the office. To accomplish this goal, Ms. Chavez constructs the scale shown in Table 5.9 and has each of Julio's teachers rate his behavior at each class.

Table 5.8 **Example five–point scale for lying behavior**

Behavior	Indicators				
	A	B	C	D	F
The student will tell the truth when responding to the teacher	Reacts to redirection without argument	Tells the truth when questioned by the teacher	Lying with retraction	Lying without Retraction	Lying with shut down

Table 5.9 **Example five-point scale for aggressive behavior**

Behavior	Indicators				
	A	B	C	D	F
The student will respect others physical space, and not act aggressively toward peers	Respectful of others' physical space	Looking at others aggressively, but far enough away to not physically invade others space	Invading others space or looking at others aggressively in close proximity	Pushing or assertively bumping others	Pushing or bumping others AND initiating a physical fight

Guttman Scales

A Guttman scale is a set of items with dichotomous (for example Yes or No) answers. A Guttman scale arranges items in an order so that an individual who agrees with a particular item also agrees with items of lower rank-order. Agreement with any one item implies agreement with the lower-order items (Crocker & Algina, 2008).

Guttman scales have the potential to be used in attitude inventories or in content areas where skills are cumulative. For example, in mathematics one assumes that if an examinee can successfully answer more difficult items (such as summing two three-digit numbers), they would be able to answer the easier questions (such as summing two two-digit numbers) (Crocker & Algina, 2008).

The Guttmann scale has the potential to overestimate reliability due to the lack of sensitivity available using a dichotomous scale for each item. The assumption that an examinee understands less difficult content creates the potential to misunderstand the examinees skill-set. An important objective in Guttman scaling is to maximize the reproducibility of response patterns from a single score (Crocker & Algina, 2008).

Thurstone Scaling

Thurstone scaling is a method of measuring attitudes along a single dimension by having the examinee indicate that they agree or disagree with a set of statements. In this type of scale, statements are designed to be parallel in construction and range from strongly positive through neutral to strongly negative (Guilford, 1954).

To create a Thurstone type scale, a large set of statements are sorted by a group of judges into eleven categories. Categories are assumed to appear equally spaced on the attitude continuum, according to how favorable the statements are towards the attitude. Items that yield the highest level of agreement among the judges as to their scale position, and that collectively represent an adequate range of contents and scale positions, are then selected for the final scale. Respondents to the scale endorse just those items with which they agree, and an individual respondent's score is calculated as the mean of the items endorsed.

Such scores are assumed to be analyzed on an interval scale of measurement (Guilford, 1954).

Once the scale is constructed, one must consider the measurement schedule.

When to Assess

Teachers often wonder when and how often data collection is required for effective behavior progress monitoring. Student behavior is often variable and inconsistent through the day. Selection of a schedule to assess can vary depending on the teacher, student, and setting. For example, students in middle or high school may have multiple classes with multiple teachers and the selection for monitoring may occur differently and represent each class period or blocks of classes depending on the needs of the student behavior and teachers' ability to perform the ratings (Vannest et al., 2010).

Monitoring needs to be consistent, active and the monitoring schedules need to reflect the students' needs (Horner & Sprague, 2010). By meeting these guidelines, decision making will improve on student behavior due to access to regular and accurate information (Horner et al., 2010). Monitoring that occurs three or more times a day produces higher effect sizes than less frequent monitoring and monitoring intervals of one or two hours are more reliable than intervals of half a day (Vannest et. al 2010).

What Are Measurement Schedules?

Monitoring is the process of observing and recording scaled behaviors or expectations for the purpose of feedback or decision making. The monitoring schedule is the frequency of data collected using a behavior scale. Campus personnel have flexibility in choosing when and how often to monitor student behavior. Effective behavior progress monitoring relies on collecting data on the same behaviors at the same times every day.

Why We Need to Create Monitoring Schedules

Collecting data on a set schedule allows teachers to evaluate changes in the behavior rather than changes in the environment or behavioral demands. If behavioral data is collected and compared from different times during the day then other unknown influences may contribute to the behavior change. To control these potential influences and create a complete picture of the student's behavior, data must be collected in a consistent way.

Sensitivity Versus Feasibility

Recording data on student behavior is known to be a significant barrier to effective progress monitoring. Teachers often have difficulty finding time to disengage from the class in order to perform this task. It is a balance for teachers to accurately record student data and fulfill all other classroom duties. On one hand, the more data a teacher can record the more sensitive the data as a whole will be to behavior changes in the classroom. For example, if the student only breaks a certain rule during one period per day, a morning/afternoon monitoring schedule will not be sensitive enough to these behaviors. By examining the data one would be given the impression that the behavior occurs all morning rather than only during a certain period. A general guideline for behavior progress monitoring is that the more problematic the student's behavior is, the more data is necessary to accurately describe the behavior. Remember that data on student behavior is designed to offer additional insight beyond simple intuition. Through the data-recording and evaluation process, teachers may discover more information about the behavior, which will lead to intervention in a more timely and efficient manner.

Conclusion

Measurement should be approached in a thoughtful and deliberate manner. Organization and planning in measurement can help to create quality assessment tools that illuminate valuable information about the test taker's skill or behavior. The results of these measures may have an important impact on the student's educational process.

The student's access to educational opportunities often hinge on his or her ability to produce satisfactory scores on various measures. Those who have the charge of creating these measurement tools should be mindful of the potential importance of the scores.

6

INTEROBSERVER/RATER RELIABILITY

All data requires reliability for usefulness. Direct observation data such as is commonly used in SCR requires interobserver or interrater reliability. This chapter includes a discussion of up-to-date methods for calculating reliability for a variety of scales. Dichotomous scales and multi category scales require different calculations. For example a "yes/no" scale such as "Did Chris follow school rules?" can only be an agree/disagree and simple agreement and Kappa Linear weight will handle this calculation. On the other hand, a four-point scale to assess to what degree Chris followed school rules (almost never, sometimes, often, almost always) will have degrees of "miss" and an agree/disagree calculation will not be as sensitive. Practical considerations such as when to use a variety of calculations is covered in this chapter.

What is Reliability and Why is it Important?

Single Case Research hinges on measurement quality. The sources of error in measurement (both known and unknown) are exacerbated under the microscope of a focus on an individual yet may be difficult to articulate if only a visual analysis is used. A visual analysis assumes that error in measurement is controlled or somewhat controlled when a baseline is stable. There are, however, two sources of error—random and systematic. If a baseline is not long enough it may not account for random error and depending on the reliability and validity of the measurement it may not account for systematic error. For example, a five-session baseline may miss how an environment changes over a period of time (randomly or systematically). Design features are expected to minimize threats to internal validity but can only account for random errors in measure, systematic errors such as bias and/or drift would likely not be controlled via design.

Measurement quality can be evaluated through the concept of reliability. "Reliability being a fundamental characteristic of measurement" (Franklin, Allison, & Gorman, 1997, p. 50; Ghiselli, Campbell, & Zedeck, 1981). If I were in a grocery store measuring four apples on a scale, how exact would that measure be and how "accurate" would that measurement be in relationship to the "reality" of how much the apples weigh? We expect a certain degree of measurement error in our daily lives. We are typically comfortable with a little variation in a scale, or a give-or-take measurement error when the news reports on survey results; even the amount of rainfall we get is probably not subjected to a desire or expectation of perfect measurement. When is error in measurement too much, though? When does a measure go from reliable or acceptable, to unreliable and unacceptable? At some point the error around a measure has a negative impact. Since we are paying for apples by weight, we may allow a tolerance of a few ounces or a few pennies, but probably not a half a pound or several dollars. We may be happy with a personal weight scale being a pound or two off, but how about five, ten, or twenty? We would likely recalibrate or throw it away, and if the rainfall is reported at several inches and we are standing ankle deep in water in the living room, we may question the source of the data. Unreliable data means unreliable decisions, a situation to be avoided in working with vulnerable populations.

An aspect of reliable measurement is precision. Figure 6.1 illustrates related issues regarding accuracy and precision in measurement. We use it here to illustrate the differences in error. In the first diagram the true value (black cross) and the scores or observations (black dots) are reasonably similar. In the next diagram, the blue dots are falling within a reasonable parameter to the "real" score or actual event so the observations are accurate in that they still represent "reality" but they are not "precise." In the following two illustrations you see demonstrated precision (all scores are close to each other) but they are not precise, followed by a demonstration of neither accuracy nor precision.

Now imagine this is human behavior. An example of accurate and precise measurement would be if 200 SIBs occurred in a day and all

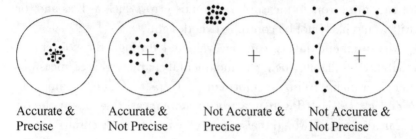

| Accurate & | Accurate & | Not Accurate & | Not Accurate & |
| Precise | Not Precise | Precise | Not Precise |

Figure 6.1 **Example of accuracy and precision. Adapted from www.more steam.com/toolbox/measurement-system-analysis.cfm**

observers repeatedly scored near 200— for example scores such as 199, 198, 195, 205, and 211. These scores are close both to reality and to each other, indicating precise and accurate scores. The reverse (measurement that was neither accurate nor precise) would be if observers recorded scores such as 150, 100, 350, and 850. These scores are neither accurate (not close to reality) nor precise (not close to each other).

Sources of Error in Reliability

Measurement error is the difference between the "real" (actual, true) value and the "obtained" (recorded, observed, gained, acquired, reported) value. All measurement in an applied setting will have error (Hofmann, 2005). Error is either random, meaning it is caused by unknown or unpredictable changes, or error is systematic—meaning it happens the same way to the same degree, likely related to the measure itself.

Random errors are more easily detected than systematic errors. Random errors can push scores up or down (either way) systematic errors occur in the "same" direction and because those errors are patterned they are more difficult to detect because the data will appear to make sense.

Reliability can be assessed via multiple observers (interrater reliability). Multiple observations (internal consistency), multiple occasions (temporal consistency/test–retest reliability). Reliability improves when the number of samples (or sampling events) increases. With equivalent repeated measurements, the more likely it is that one will replicate results. With replicable results it is less likely that these results are caused by error. Alternatively, in progress monitoring, the repeated measure of growth would demonstrate consistency in pattern, for example a daily sample is likely to be more reliable than a weekly sample.

Sources of Error are Known and Unknown

There are many known sources of error which can produce systematic error in the data. As a brief review for the interested reader we list several here. Error threatens the accuracy of the data, and thus interferes with our ability to make decisions.

- *Discrimination*   This is the ability to "tell the difference" between one event and the next. For example, was the student on task or off task?
- *Resolution/clarity*   Occurs when the observer may not have physically "seen" the entire event or series of events.
- *Lack of linearity*   This is related to the consistency of the bias in a rater. One inconsistent rater is difficult to align with another consistent rater. For example a teacher who consistently rates harshly is a "known" source of error, a teacher who rates randomly (sometimes harsh sometimes not) is more difficult to get agreement with when rating.
- *Instrumentation*   Anything related to equipment or supplies may interfere with accurate data. For example timers, batteries, mechanics, running out of pencil lead, running out of paper, or where an observer doesn't have a previously-devised data collection sheet and therefore creates their own.
- *Dependency or hysteresis*   This source of error is related to the individual's performance based on the environment (so, for example, the teacher doesn't follow protocol, or the student is sick).
- *Rater error*   People can make mistakes in coding, seeing categories, understanding the definitions, or simply do not do well in training.
- *Drift*   A rater may experience a slow change away from the standard over time.

One way to characterize error is to identify a confidence interval or a confidence band. We might say "I'm 95 percent certain" in daily life when making a judgment. When using data in schools, identifying a confidence interval with which we are comfortable is dependent in part on the decision (low stakes or high stakes). If I am using SCR data to determine if a child needs special education services, I had better be confident in the accuracy of my data. A 95 percent confidence level is probably necessary perhaps even 99 percent. If on the other hand, I am determining if a child should be a part of a tutoring group for the week, and the decision is revisited weekly, an 80 percent confidence interval may be sufficient. A standard deviation can be used as a way to quantify the uncertainty. A large standard deviation in relation to the score represents more uncertainty. A small standard deviation in relation to the score represents less uncertainty (Figure 6.2).

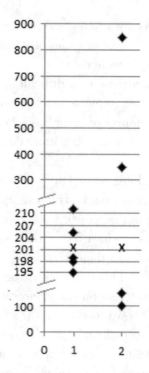

Figure 6.2 **Data illustrating high accuracy in group 1 and low accuracy in group 2. Optimal accuracy is indicated by the "X" in both groups.**

Some Terms and Exercises for Interested Readers

- *Standard deviation*   This is a measure of variability in scores (how close scores are to the mean). A standard deviation is the square root of its variance.

ACTIVITY

1. Take your baseline scores and find the mean. Example: 3, 4, 4, 1 = a mean of 12/4= 3.
2. Subtract each individual score from the mean and square it $(3-3)^2$, $(4-3)^2$ and so on.
3. Take these new values and find the mean.
4. Voila—the standard deviation (of a population). Now do this for a "sample" of your own student data and see what it tells you.

- *Standard error*   This is the standard deviation of the sampling distribution of a statistic (a statistic is a calculation about the scores, for example a mean is a statistic). If my obtained measures are 3,4,4, and 1 and they average 3, then the sample is 3,4,4,1 and the statistic is 3 (the mean).
- *Confidence interval*   The estimate of the interval around observations. A confidence interval is related to the population parameter (a "population" is all of the scores). This is different to an estimation because it is calculated from observations or scores. What this means is that if many experiments were to occur, they would be likely to have a result in this same range. This is not an absolute certainty but a probability.

Addressing Systematic Error: Ensuring Reliability, or Minimizing Threats to Reliability.

The threats to the reliability of data are many. To minimize threats to reliability you should be aware of those listed above and consider how to control for them or address them—particularly in high-stakes or potentially contentious cases. For example to tackle errors of instrumentation, you should be certain that timers have fresh batteries or are charged, provide data collectors with more than one instrument to write with, and train raters to not self-create recording forms but to reschedule data collection if they forget necessary materials. In dealing with the potential for drift errors, you might have observers re-train to a standard after a certain number of trials to ensure the criterion remains the same. Prepared and thoughtful data collection which includes training should produce reliable results, but a second observer for 20 percent of recordings is required for defensible data. If data is taken Monday to Friday, one day of that week necessitates a second rater and a comparison of those scores. If 20 hours of data are collected, four of those hours need to be represented by a second rater. This rating by two independent individuals (both with the same training and same opportunity to observe) is compared by calculating interrater, also called interobserver, reliability.

Calculating Interrater or Interobserver Reliability

Several indices exist to calculate interrater reliability. The most widely used for direct observation count data or multi-category scales with ordinal level data is percent agreement (Suen & Lee, 1985). Percent agreement is an examination of whether or not there is a direct match between two raters' scores.

If Stacey and I both count the number of times Judy hits herself in ten minutes and Stacey counts eight and I count ten we are in agreement 80 percent of the time.

Agreement / Agreement + Disagreement or
8 / 8 + 2 or 8 / 10 = 80%

If Stacey and I are using intervals rather than counts and there are 15 intervals during this observation the score might look like this: 3 agreements / 3 agreements + 9 disagreements = 3 / 12 or 25 percent.

Regardless of how we are measuring there is always the possibility that some number of those agreements are a result of chance. For

Table 6.1 **Example of agreement coding over 15 intervals**

Participant	Intervals														
	1	2	3	4	5	6	7	8	9	10	11	12	13	14	15
Stacey	x	x	x		x		x		x	x		x			
Kim	x			x		x	x	x		x	x		x	x	x

example, if Stacey and I are scoring how well Judy behaved during math using an indicator such as "followed all classroom rules" and our score was either a "yes" or a "no," Stacey and I would have a 50 percent opportunity to agree based just on chance. Fortunately there are calculations that will account for chance such as Cohen's Kappa (Cohen, 1960) and Linear Weighted Kappa (Fleiss & Cohen, 1973), or Cramer's V (Cramer, 1980). Cohen's Kappa and Linear Weighted Kappa can be calculated if the scale has between two and eight categories using a free online source from Vassar College (Lowry, 2010). Using the website you select the number of categories ("yes/no" is two for example, ABCDF is five). Then complete the data entry matrix: "A" and "B" are the two observers (for example, teacher is A, and school psychologist is B) and the numbers are the categories on the scale. Then select "calculate"—Cohen's Kappa (shown as Unweighted Observed Kappa) and the hybrid Linear Weighted Kappa (shown as Weighted Observed Kappa) are computed instantly.

These calculations address exact agreement, and Kappa or Kappa Linear Weight will handle "chance" but what about a near-miss agreement? Let's say that Stacey and I are observing John teasing Lauren in class. We don't want to count "teasing" because sometimes the teasing is worse than others and since we are graphing and charting John's behavior in order to work with him to improve it, we want to show the dimensions of teasing. Therefore we determine to create a scale that reflects the full range from light teasing up to really horrible bullying. Assume that we (Stacey and I) met with the team of teachers and parents, and maybe even John and Lauren; we are all in agreement about teasing being a problem and we create the seven point scale shown in Table 6.2.

Table 6.2 **Seven Point Scale**

1	2	3	4	5	6	7
No teas- ing	Teasing glances and looks	Looking and making funny faces or gestures, like sticking out a tongue or waving inappro- priately	Calling names or echolalia e.g. Lauren says "stop it" and John says "stop it"	Inappro- priate proximity	Physical threat, "I'm going to get you" or "I'm going to find you"	Bullying, threaten- ing, inti- midation, physical proximity, doesn't stop when told

If Stacey and I are rating John's teasing/bullying and she rates his behavior at a three and I give him a two, we have zero agreement. Was our score unreliable, however? Can we use this measure? Teasing glances is pretty close to looking and pulling funny faces— can we somehow count the fact that a two and a three are close to one another? This may not be exact agreement but surely it is different from Stacey scoring John's behavior as a two, and my giving him a seven—so can we take this into account? The answer is yes, we can.

This issue is called closeness of approximation and there are several indices we could use, including Pearson's contingency coefficient (Pearson CC) (Goodman, Leo, & Kruskal, 1954, 1959, 1963, 1972), Kendall's tau-b (Kendall, 1938), and Pearson's r (Fisher, 1915).

Pearson's r can be calculated in Microsoft Excel more than one way. The first method is to type the formula into the desired cell beginning with = PEARSON followed by the range of scores for each rater separated by a comma in parenthesis (see Figure 6.3). The second method is to select the Formulas tab, More Functions, Statistical, and scroll down to click on PEARSON. You will be asked which arrays (cell ranges for each observer) you would like to use. You may either type in the ranges or you may drag the mouse to select the ranges under each of the arrays. Select OK and a Pearson's r will be calculated.

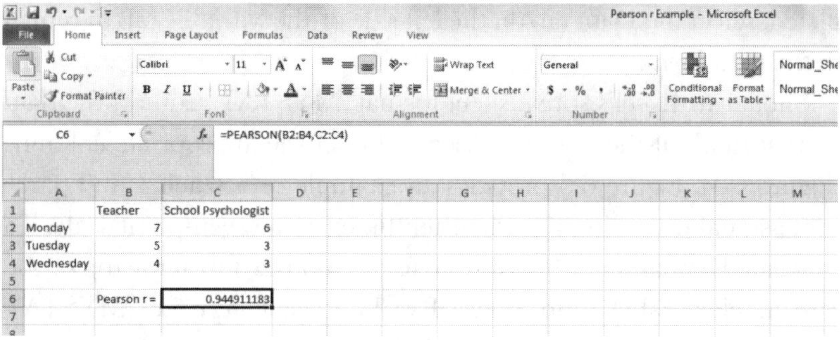

Figure 6.3 **Calculating R in Excel.**

The overall best index to use for calculating reliability (Parker, Vannest, & Davis, in press), however, is Kendall's tau-b. Kendall's tau-b is the most reliable index and can be calculated using MYSTAT (SYSTAT, 2008).

The first step to calculate Kendall's tau-b in MYSTAT is to go under the Untitled1.syz tab and the Variable tab at the bottom of the page to change the variable names to the names of observers under the column Variable Name (see Arrows in Figure 6.4). When com-

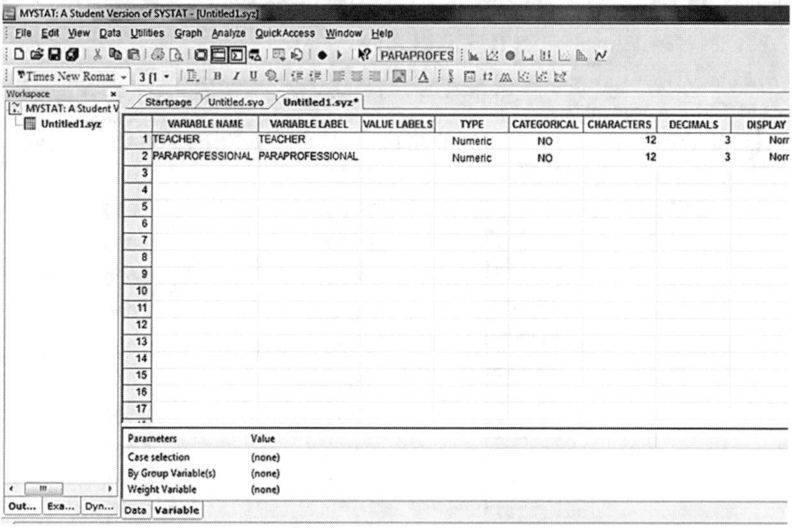

Figure 6.4 **Example data between teacher and paraprofessional.**

pleted, select the Data tab on the left side of the Variable tab to return to the data form.

Similar to Excel's spreadsheet format, MYSTAT requires the data analyst to input the observers' scores under the appropriate columns (Figure 6.4). Figure 6.5 provides an example of a teacher and paraprofessional observing a student ten times on a seven-point scale. To calculate Kendall's tau-b simply go to the Analyze tab at the top of the screen, select Tables, and choose Two-Way (see Figure 6.6). MYSTAT creates a cross-tabulation matrix similar to the Vassar College website and requires a Row Variable (rater 1) and a Column Variable (rater 2); select one rater and select Add to Row Variable and the other rater to Column Variable (see Figure 6.7). Under the Measures tab, select only Kendall's tau-b before clicking on OK (see Figure 6.8). The reliability score will be found below Value under the title "Measures of Association for TEACHER and PARAPROFESSIONAL."

Depending on the type of measurement you are using, and the context of the data, you must first identify if you need "exact match"

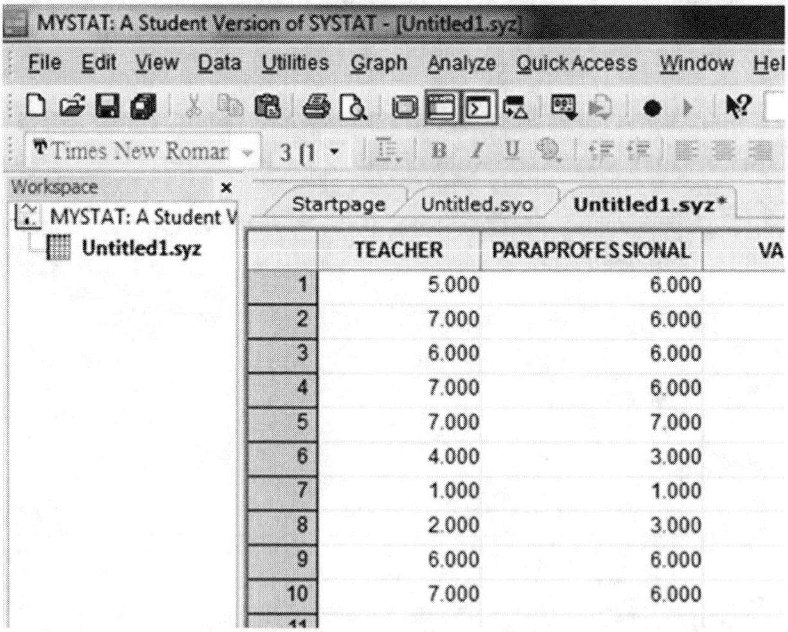

	TEACHER	PARAPROFESSIONAL	VA
1	5.000	6.000	
2	7.000	6.000	
3	6.000	6.000	
4	7.000	6.000	
5	7.000	7.000	
6	4.000	3.000	
7	1.000	1.000	
8	2.000	3.000	
9	6.000	6.000	
10	7.000	6.000	

Figure 6.5 **Example display of data set up for analysis.**

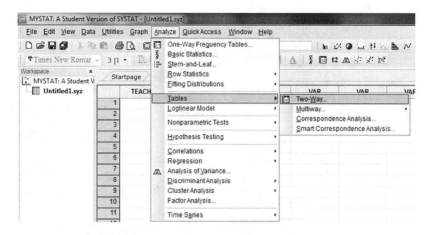

Figure 6.6 **Screen shot from Crosstabs in MYSTAT to set up agreement matrix.**

Figure 6.7 **Screen shot from Crosstabs in MYSTAT to set up agreement matrix.**

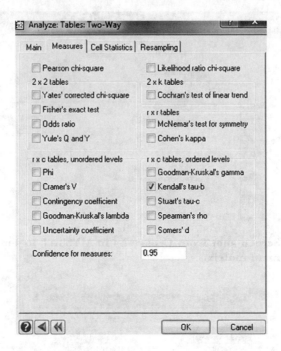

Figure 6.8 **Screen shot from Crosstabs in MYSTAT to calculate tau-b.**

or "closeness of approximation." If you value or prefer an exact match (and you have four or fewer choices on your scale) then use Cramer's V or Cohen's Kappa, to minimize chance effects inflating your data. If however, you want to give some credit for close scores and account for "how closely they agreed on the scale (for example if one teacher has rated the student's behavior a four and the other a five) then use Kendall's tau-b.

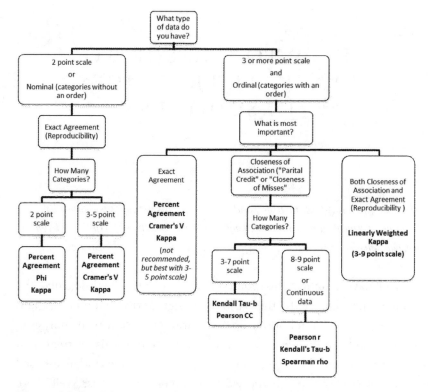

Figure 6.9 **Decision model for choosing appropriate reliability.**

Reprinted from Smith, S.L., Vannest, K.J. & Davis, J.L. Seven Reliability indices for high-stakes decision making: Description, selection, and simple calculation. *Psychology in the Schools, 40(10),* 2011.

7

HOW TO USE SCR TO
EVALUATE PRACTICES
IN SCHOOLS

This chapter provides practical examples—a step-by-step review of considerations like measurement, data collection, length of phases, clarity of effects and control, design considerations, calculating effect size, and reliability of measures.

If you have reached this point in the book you have learned the context for using SCR, the basics of design and visual analysis, and the state of the art in bottom-up non-parametric, statistical analysis in order to determine effect sizes and confidence intervals for treatment effectiveness, and in aggregating studies to determine evidence-based practices. So how do you apply this knowledge in schools? Well, there are two opportunities to use this information. The first is at the client level and the second is at the program level. When we say client level, we mean decisions regarding outcomes for an individual. When we say program level, we mean the combinations of data which could be used to determine that a combination of treatments, placements, and interventions is effective for an individual or a group. To illustrate these scenarios we will use three cases.

CASE 1

Lewan is a ninth-grade girl with attendance problems and failing grades in most core classes. She has a DSM diagnosis of ADHD NOS, and Conduct Disorder. Her full score IQ is in the normal range. Lewan receives support services from Special Education. Lewan accesses services through a "content-mastery" room for testing and study skills and the decision-making team at school is meeting to determine if Lewan would be better served by providing her with more special education time for instruction of content-area course-work specifically for Language Arts, Western Civilization, and Algebra.

Using single case research to make this decision provides some defensibility to the data. The team uses the following planning guide (shown in Figure 7.1) to lead them through decisions of question formation, design determination, measurement selection, data collection schedule, reliability and analysis.

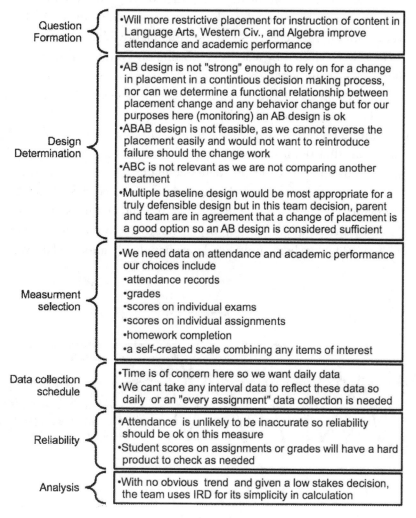

Figure 7.1 **Guiding questions for single case design application to Case 1.**

This data was collected in a AB design. Attendance is scored as a present/absent and added to score from a zero to a score of three (attended all classes). Homework in this example is assigned every day in every class so 0–3 is also the score range. If homework were not an every-day, every-class occurrence, then a percentage would be needed to standardize the score across the classes so that on days when one homework is the maximum score, scoring a one would reflect 100 percent and not one out of three. Average daily grade is scored as a number: one is the value of an F and five is the value of an A. The average for all three classes is reported (see Figure 7.2).

Data was collected by teachers reporting on Lewan's performance after each class using the email system. The school psychologist enters the data into an Excel spread sheet for record keeping. In this example, the last four days of Lewan's school performance were used as baseline data and her schedule was changed on a Friday with data collected daily from that point forward, rather than to maintain Lewan in a failing scenario while collecting data (see Figure 7.2).

A visual analysis indicates that attendance in three classes may be improving but the data is so variable that it is difficult to say for sure. Homework completion has improved from the zero rates in baseline as reported by teachers, and attendance has clearly improved as well.

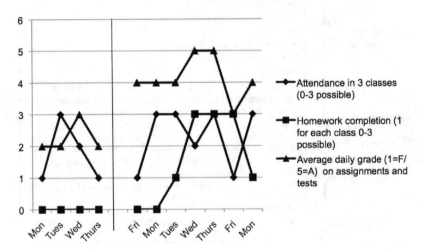

Figure 7.2 **Data for Lewan on attendance, homework and average daily grade.**

Since there is no baseline trend present and this decision-making scenario is fairly low-stakes (everyone on the team is in agreement, the decision to change Lewan's schedule will be revisited frequently, and the change has no potential harmful consequences given that Lewan is currently failing all classes and not attending regularly), an effect size analysis is a more academic exercise but may be useful in particular for determining if attendance rates have changed. So a metric like IRD (improvement rate difference) is straightforward to calculate.

CASE 2

Charlie is a second grade child with suspected Autism Spectrum Disorder, and a diagnosis of PDD from preschool but no new evaluation data. Charlie is not receiving instruction in special education classrooms, but he remains on the special education service rolls as a child who is "monitored." He demonstrates challenges in transition times, noticeable self-stimulation behaviors, he has difficulty making eye-contact and few social relationships. Charlie is good at academics and excels in classes with high structure and individual assignments like independent assignments at his desk, or reading and completing worksheet tasks. Charlie resists leaving assignments to go to the cafeteria for lunch or engage in breaks on the playground, choosing instead to remain indoors and work. The school psychologist, counselor and second-grade teacher hope to maintain Charlie's education in the general education population. Charlie's parents wonder if more individual assistance would be helpful in reducing self-stimulation behaviors and increasing the time spent in social interaction with non-disabled peers. The school team would like to compare a 1:1 aide with the use of a peer-buddy arrangement as the school team believes the adult aid will be more stigmatizing (not to mention more expensive).

The same guiding questions we used in Case 1 (Lewan) can be used to structure a single case design to answer questions about the relative effects of these program changes for Charlie (see Figure 7.3).

In this example we want to compare the effects of using an adult aide with the effects of using a peer buddy. Although you could compare adult aide to baseline and peer buddy to baseline, that would ignore the adjacent phase treatment of adult aide and we cannot

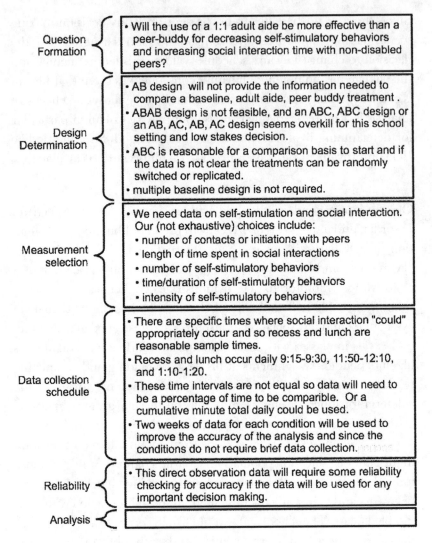

Question Formation
- Will the use of a 1:1 adult aide be more effective than a peer-buddy for decreasing self-stimulatory behaviors and increasing social interaction time with non-disabled peers?

Design Determination
- AB design will not provide the information needed to compare a baseline, adult aide, peer buddy treatment .
- ABAB design is not feasible, and an ABC, ABC design or an AB, AC, AB, AC design seems overkill for this school setting and low stakes decision.
- ABC is reasonable for a comparison basis to start and if the data is not clear the treatments can be randomly switched or replicated.
- multiple baseline design is not required.

Measurement selection
- We need data on self-stimulation and social interaction. Our (not exhaustive) choices include:
  - number of contacts or initiations with peers
  - length of time spent in social interactions
  - number of self-stimulatory behaviors
  - time/duration of self-stimulatory behaviors
  - intensity of self-stimulatory behaviors.

Data collection schedule
- There are specific times where social interaction "could" appropriately occur and so recess and lunch are reasonable sample times.
- Recess and lunch occur daily 9:15-9:30, 11:50-12:10, and 1:10-1:20.
- These time intervals are not equal so data will need to be a percentage of time to be comparible. Or a cumulative minute total daily could be used.
- Two weeks of data for each condition will be used to improve the accuracy of the analysis and since the conditions do not require brief data collection.

Reliability
- This direct observation data will require some reliability checking for accuracy if the data will be used for any important decision making.

Analysis

Figure 7.3 **Guiding questions for a single case design.**

ignore the impact this may have had on the subsequent treatment (see Figures 7.4 and 7.5). One design option would be to reintroduce baseline and then use a peer buddy, or to use repeated treatments.

In this example we will calculate IRD for an AB comparison of baseline to adult aide and BC comparison of adult aide to peer buddy. For social interaction baseline data there is one data point which is "improved" or overlapping out of the 10 data points, giving $1/10 =$

Time	Social Interaction (% time)	Self-Stimulation (% time)
1	20	35
2	46	60
3	24	58
4	52	72
5	12	40
6	39	55
7	15	34
8	23	43
9	34	56
10	22	29
11	50	30
12	55	23
13	60	43
14	65	36
15	50	20
16	89	12
17	50	18
18	66	24
19	62	30
20	80	10
21	90	15
22	95	7
23	74	3
24	88	19
25	93	40
26	98	20
27	88	15
28	85	38
29	85	22
30	65	9

Figure 7.4 **Guiding questions for single case design application to Case 2.**

10 percent. In the intervention of an adult aide there is no data to be removed so $10/10=100$ resulting in an improvement rate difference of $100-10$ or 90 percent. To make this calculation more robust, we should distribute that one data point across both phases so we use $0.5/10$ and a $9.5/10$ for a 0.05 and a 0.95. We see that $0.95-0.05 = 0.90$ as well so IRD for Adult aid is 90 in both scenarios. In this example IRD is the same but depending on the data, your results will sometimes differ slightly.

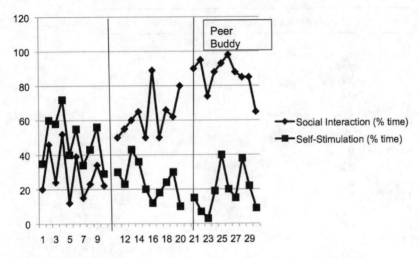

Figure 7.5 **Graph of data for Charlie across three conditions.**

Calculating IRD for the comparison of peer buddy to adult aide we need to remove two data points to eliminate the overlap. This could be two from the A phase 2/10 and 0 from the B phase or 10/10 leaving an IRD of 100−20 or 80 percent. OR a robust calculation would be a 1/10 and a 9/10 or 90−10 which in this case is also an 80 percent IRD.

An adult aide in this scenario is slightly more effective (90 percent compared to 80 percent) to a peer buddy. In the given example, both 90 percent and 80 percent improvement is a large change. The team may then determine that the additional costs of an adult aide for an additional 10 percent gain is not warranted, not economical and possibly the 80 percent change is socially significant enough that the team may determine to use a peer buddy. Using data to demonstrate changes in behavior, but also comparative treatment effects is a valuable use of time.

CASE 3

Isaiah is a second grade pupil and is in the process of special education referral. The district where Isaiah goes to school uses an RTI process to establish a need for comprehensive evaluation. Isaiah's data is needed to document his progress in reading, his responsiveness to small group instruction and his time on task.

The same guiding questions (see Figure 7.6) are used by the team to establish Isaiah's responsiveness to the intervention they deem "small group instruction."

In this scenario, the AB design demonstrates a change in both time on task and reading fluency with the onset of the small group instruction (Table 7.1). We cannot determine if this is a functional relationship, but we can say that change occurred, and given the change in slope for reading (see Figure 7.7) we have a different prediction for

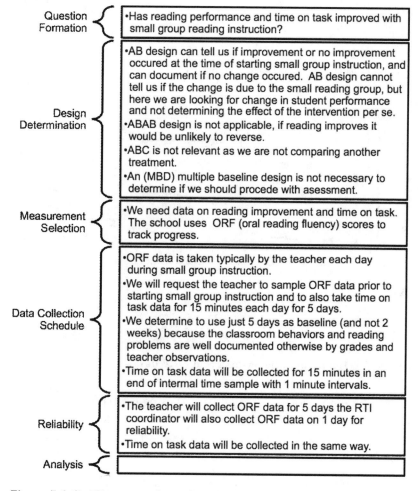

Figure 7.6 **Guiding questions for single case design application to Case 3.**

Table 7.1 Raw data for ORF and Time on Task Measures

Day	ORF	Time on Task
M	32	67
T	33	67
W	33	73
Th	34	73
F	35	80
M	53	86
T	55	86
W	58	86
Th	59	86
F	62	93

Note: Abbreviation ORF = oral reading fluency

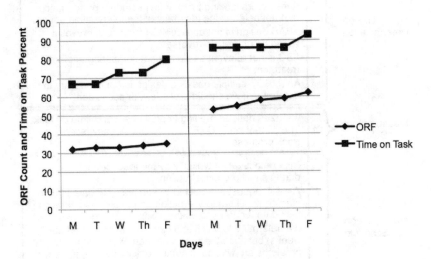

Figure 7.7 **Graph of time on-task and ORF data.**

future student performance than we did using the baseline data. The team may determine that small group instruction is warranted and should be continued rather than deciding to begin a comprehensive assessment.

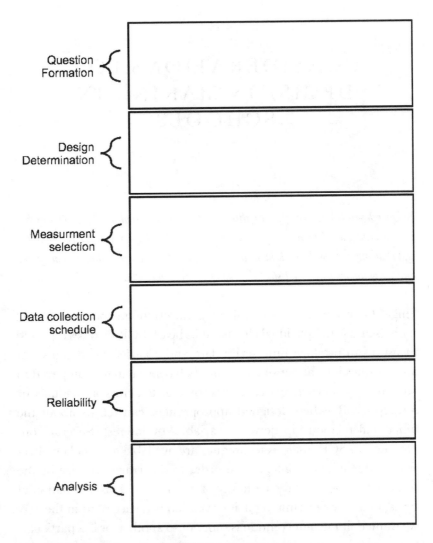

Figure 7.8 **Template for SCR design.**

These three examples provide just a glimpse at the flexibility of single case research designs for use in school settings and school-related decision making.

The guiding questions provided above can be used to structure meetings and a blank template is provided in Figure 7.8.

8

CONSIDERATIONS FOR DECISION MAKING IN SCHOOLS

Judging defensibility, evaluating quality of data or existing evidence, how to strengthen existing data and when not to use it are the topics of this chapter. We discuss the values and challenges of SCR work in schools and applied settings providing a step by step practice guide for how to get started in using SCR in the field.

Single Case Research is useful for a variety of purposes in school settings and with individual clients. At its heart, SCR involves repeated measures to produce time series data and a variety of designs can answer questions about one or more behavior changes compared to baseline, or alternative treatments, or effects across individuals or settings. SCR, when designed appropriately, can tell us about the functional relationship between variables of interest. Several non-parametric, SCR analysis techniques are available to calculate effect sizes and confidence intervals in order to determine the size of the behavior change and the certainty of our results. This calculation of ES is useful for determining if intervention was successful in the way we wanted, if one intervention is superior to another, or if a particular practice or intervention is evidence based.

This book has walked the reader through an overview and history of what SCR is and how to engage in SCR design and analysis, discussed issues related to data collection, and concluded by providing exemplars of some application cases. This last chapter is dedicated to understanding the difference between the more typical way of looking at assessment quality (Classic Test Theory or CTT) and presenting an alternative which is better suited for the qualities of time series data, namely TSLR or Time Series Fixed Linear Regression. TSLR captures measurement error more comprehensively than CTT (Parker, Vannest, Davis, Clemens, 2012).

For school psychologists or other professionals involved in the administration and interpretation of assessments in schools, the use of time series data for decisions which are irrevocable or otherwise critical in nature requires some new understandings to accurately summarize scores. These skills are unlikely to be taught in existing graduate course work based on the classic test theory measurement model. Yet these skills are important for understanding the defensibility of the data and some of the issues involved in decision making based on data. Just because it is a number or in a graph doesn't mean it provides any level of justifiable information.

We believe there are several aspect of understanding progress monitoring assessment or time series data which will generate more defensibility in our decision making. The first is the estimation of a static performance level in PM at a fixed point in time. Next is an understanding of the fit between the needed level of confidence and the "stakes" involved in an educational decision. Third is the understanding of how and when to express measurement error for an estimated score. Fourth, the requisites for judging reliable improvement between two points in time. Fifth, the differences between slope and trendedness, and which is applicable when. Sixth, how do we express "rate of improvement" (slope) with error, and last the controlling of autocorrelation. Mastery of these skills should improve our use of data in decision making.

- *Estimating a static performance level in PM* Static performance is another name for data which represents a "point in time." Static data is useful for determining how well or poorly a student is doing currently or was doing at a point in the past. Student data in loosely-controlled school settings is rarely absolutely stable or perfectly trended. Instead data is very typically "bouncy" and may be difficult to visually interpret. In addition each data point contains error.

In Figure 8.1 we represent two methods for determining static performance. The first method is called "multiple trials" in regression.

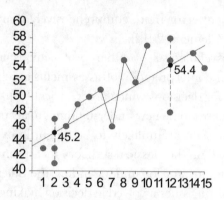

Figure 8.1 **Two methods for obtaining a static performance estimate.**

The second is "approximate repeats." The multiple trials method uses multiple probes, rather than just one—this could be as few as three or even two —and these scores are entered individually (not averaged). See data point 2 in Figure 8.1 (data values 41, 43, 47). The best estimate of performance at data point 2 is neither the median nor the mean (43 and 43.67 respectively) but the point on the trend line (45.2). This value is an "estimated score," also known as "Y-est" or "Y-hat." You can get this score in a normal output from a linear regression model, its value based on the three probes of that day but also all the other scores in the series. This improves the precision of a static performance estimate and the score is more stable.

The second method is "approximate repeats." As in the first method "multiple trials," approximate repeats uses three or more adjacent scores. In our example at week 12 we identify week 11 and week 13 as adjacent scores. Each of these scores is then entered on the median value (12). Each score is entered individually. The best estimated score of static performance is represented by the dot on the line (54.4).

The point on the regression line is a Y-hat or Y-est score and this is the best estimate of performance at a fixed point in time because the error is based on a small group of scores, rather than just one score. Text in business, physical science, and health provide multiple examples of these methods (Neter, Kutner, Nachtsheim, & Wasserman, 1996; Graybill & Iyer, 1998; Draper & Smith, 1998; Armitage, Berry & Matthews, 2002).

- *Fitting a level of confidence to an educational decision*   Remember that most classroom decisions about instructional changes, minor modifications or grades do not need to consider measurement error. Some decisions, however, are "high-stakes," such as retaining a child or providing special education services. This level of decision making requires additional information about a score representing a child's performance. This level of decision making requires confidence intervals around the data to express our certainty in the score, and our estimate of the error. The first step is to determine the lowest level of confidence we are willing to accept. For example are we comfortable with 50 percent certainty? Probably not, but what about 80 percent certainty? It probably depends on the decision. If we are determining whether or not to remove a student from a comprehensive campus and place them in an alternative school or home hospital, we would probably want a 95 or even 99 percent certainty in our data.

There are costs in inaccurate decisions. For example, providing additional reading instruction before school to a student who is struggling incurs the cost of time, the potential stigma, and the opportunity costs of the social time in which the child would otherwise be engaged. These costs total a very low risk for long term problems. Therefore an 80 percent confidence interval might be reasonable. On the other hand, the determination to identify a child as disabled has high monetary costs to the system, greater psychological burden for the child and their family, and is a more permanent decision. These ramifications may lead the team to require a 95 percent level of certainty. In each case we are willing to be wrong at a certain rate. In the above examples 1 in 5 (20 percent) for reading instruction, or 1 in 20 (5 percent) for disability determination. In business and medicine, evaluating the cost associated with a decision is a common practice (Ioannidis, 2005; Djulbegovic, Hozo, Schwartz & McMasters, 1999). It may be less so in education but should be considered. Financial, psychological, social, and opportunity costs (and their reversibility) are all components of this decision. "The 95 percent level of confidence (tolerating only one erroneous decision per twenty) should be reserved for decisions with the highest risks: those with substantial social or educational impact, those with lasting impact, and those which are not easily reversible (AERA, APA & NCME, 1999)" (Parker et al., 2009).

That said, a 95 percent confidence requirement may mean that much of our classroom progress monitoring data will reflect too much error and create decision paralysis. So for practical decision making, schools should select the lowest level of confidence permissible. This risk tolerance threshold will be different for each decision. A school should not require a confidence interval a priori for all decisions such as "use 80 percent for decision making." Instead, each decision about determining level must take into account the associated cost–benefit ratio.

- *Expressing an estimated score (Y-est) with its measurement error*   We have established the need for a Y-est (known also as a confidence interval) under certain circumstances: important, serious, controversial, or irrevocable decisions. The CI is represented as a box plot or brackets around the score. These brackets represent the range of scores that could occur with equal certainty for that point in time. For example, notice in Figure 8.2 that for data point 12, the 95 percent CI represents a wider range of scores than the 80 percent CI. This should make intuitive sense. We are more certain when the range of possible scores is larger. The "true" score is somewhere between those brackets. Using data point 12 again, we are 95 percent certain the score lies between 52 and 56.8, or we are 80 percent certain the score lies between 52.9 and 55.9.

A technical note here (and interested readers may view Parker et al. 2009): progress monitoring data does not typically include multiple probes in a given day so we have demonstrated two methods for "creating" multiple probes in our first skill, multiple probes or approximate repeats. Multiple probes are required to calculate Y-est, and Y-est is the most stable estimate of a student's performance at a point in time, and not the same as error for an individual score. These are easily confused (Draper & Smith, 1998; Schwarz, 2007) and beyond the scope of this chapter but suffice it to know that the confidence interval

(CI) should not be confused with a prediction interval. PI will be greatly inflated and textbooks warn against attempting to use the PI for practical decision making with most data (Neter et al. 1996; Graybill & Iyer, 1998; Draper & Smith, 1998; Armitage, Berry & Matthews, 2002). CI is a direct output from most linear regression program outputs.

- *Judging reliable improvement from one time to a later time* Progress monitoring data is useful to compare data on performance level between two points in time to determine if the growth or change is statistically significant in the improvement. There are times when growth is measured to a criterion standard or a norm, but comparing data of an individual child to themselves is particularly useful when initial data do not conform to the norms or expected level for reasonable comparison with a criterion.

The judgment about statistically significant differences between two levels of student performance can be done visually by evaluating the two confidence intervals for overlap (Browne, 1979; Goldstein & Healy, 1995; Payton, Greenstone, & Schenker, 2003; Payton, Miller, & Raun, 2000; Schenker & Gentleman, 2001). In the case of expected growth (scores going up such as in Figure 8.3), if the upper bracket of the first score for comparison does not overlap with the lower bracket of the second score then the change or improvement is statistically significant. In order to determine a 0.05 p value or 95 percent

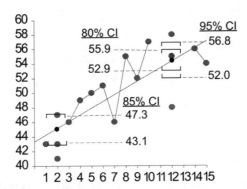

Figure 8.2 **Visual Representation of Confidence Intervals or Y-est.**

certainty, the regression program input should be set at 83.4 percent (Schenker & Gentleman, 2001). In the example (Figure 8.3) you can see confidence intervals with a 95 percent certainty established on the data we want to compare, a ten-week instructional session starting in week two and ending in week 12. The upper bracket on data point 2 has a value of 47, the lower bracket on data point 12 has a value of 52.7. These do not overlap (see the overlap check). Thus the difference is statistically significant.

- *Slope versus trendedness*   Trend line slope is calculated as rise over the run and is a typical, if not the most common performance improvement summary used in progress monitoring data. There is another option however, that is R and R^2 or trendedness. Trendedness is a better summary of growth when the comparison is between one scale type and another because slope is not a standardized index. Trendedness is also a better summary of growth when data are variable or bouncy because trendedness will reflect the consistency of the scores moving up over time. The R or R^2 will tell us the percent of score differences that are linear improvements over time. Less data consistency, less trendedness. Using both slope and trend would provide the most complete picture of the data.

This complex summary of both trend and slope do not solve the problem of scale. Slope is scale-bound and so its interpretation

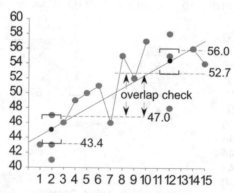

Figure 8.3 **Graphic display of *3.4 confidence intervals around designated points on the regression line.**

requires an understanding of the scale. The scale score range, the scale content, item difficulty and scale content each play a role in the interpretation of slope. For example the difference between math achievement within first grade is a different growth line than the growth across first, second, and third grade math achievement. R and R^2 are not affected by these differences in scale.

- *Rate of improvement*   Slopes, like scores, can and should be expressed with upper and lower CI boundaries at a level which is appropriately matched to the decision at stake. High stakes decisions require high degrees of certainty. CIs around a slope allow for comparison which can also inform decision making. CIs around a slope can be graphically depicted.

Figure 8.4 represents a regression slope of 0.81. The upper and lower limits pivot from a center point and represent a 95 percent confidence interval (set by using a 83.4 when calculating the regression in a statistics package). The upper bound here is 1.0 and the lower bound is 0.62.

- *Controlling autocorrelation*   Another problem with time series data is the presence of serial dependency or autocorrelation. When one data point predicts the next one undesirably, data is not independent.

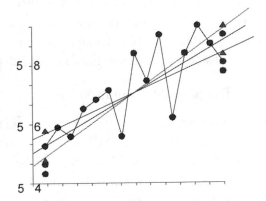

Figure 8.4 **A regression slope with upper and lower limits of the confidence interval around the slope.**

Independent data is a requirement of most statistical tests and most SCR data do not meet this requirement. A perfect linear trend is 100 percent autocorrelated but this autocorrelation is not considered harmful largely due to the expected and desired improvement of the data. So the problematic autocorrelation is that which remains after the removal of linear trend. (Busk & Marascuilo, 1988; Manolov, & Solanas, 2008; Matyas & Greenwood, 1996; Parker, Cryer & Byrns, 2005).

To solve this problem, the data is modeled, and the autocorrelation identified and then removed. This solves one problem but creates another as removal or correction can affect the initial calculation of slope and trendedness, CI, and p-values as well as the graphic depiction of the data. When problematic autocorrelation is removed ideally, there is minimum negative change and more positive gain.

Persistence in data (such as a pattern of rising and falling) is the most difficult and undesirable data to handle and may reflect problems in reliability (see previous chapters for more on this or see Salkind, 2007).

There is a free 2009 version of GRETL (GNU Regression, Econometric and Time-series Library) downloadable from http://gretl.sourceforge.net (Cottrell & Lucchetti, 2009). This package offers three methods to control autocorrelation within linear regression. All three include graphs of both original and transformed scores so the user can compare. Although actual statistical changes are successful, you will no longer be able to employ visual analysis with this transformed data if any distortion is present (Parker et al. 2009).

Decision Making in Schools

The analysis and subsequent decision making that occurs in schools is unfortunately too often bereft of data. SCR and progress monitoring data have much to offer. Practical decision requires balancing the costs of making an error (high stakes or low stakes) and the investment in collecting the data. Low-stakes decisions require fewer assurances, as inaccurate data is unlikely to cause damage. High-stakes decisions however require data with quantified reliability and data with identified levels of confidence or measurement error.

In the next decade schools will face challenges in how to monitor progress accurately and efficiently. Single case research for measuring progress and identifying best practices will certainly be one part of the answer. The quality of the design, measurement, and analysis are foundational to improved decision making and requires knowledgeable professionals in each of these arenas.

REFERENCES

Acion, L., Peterson, J., Temple, S., & Arndt, S. (2006). Probabilistic index: an intuitive non-parametric approach to measuring the size of treatment effects. *Statistics in Medicine, 25(4)*, 591–602.

Agresti, A. (1996). *An introduction to categorical data analysis.* NY: John Wiley & Sons.

Agresti, A. (2002). *Categorical data analysis* (2nd ed.). Hoboken, NJ: Wiley-Interscience.

Akritas, M.G., (2004). Nonparametric survival analysis. *Statistical Science, 19 (4)*, 615–623.

Allison, D. B. (1992). When cyclicity is a concern: a caveat regarding phase change criteria in single-case designs. *Comprehensive Mental Health Care, 2(2)*, 131–149.

Allison, D. B. & Gorman, B. S. (1993). Calculating effect sizes for meta-analysis: The case of the single case. *Behavior, Research, and Therapy, 31*, 621–631.

American Educational Research Association, American Psychological Association, and National Council on Measurement in Education (1999). *Standards for educational and psychological testing.* Washington, DC: Authors.

Andrich, D. (1978). A rating formulation for ordered response categories. *Psychometrika, 43*, 357–74.

Ardoin, S. P. & Christ, T. J. (2009). Curriculum-based measurement of oral reading: Estimates of standard error when monitoring progress using alternate passage sets. *School Psychology Review, 38*, 266–283.

Armitage, P., Berry, G., & Matthews J. N. (2002). *Statistical methods in medical research* (4th ed.). Oxford: Blackwell Science.

Baer, D. M. (1977). Perhaps it would be better not to know everything. *Journal of Applied Behavior Analysis, 10*, 167–172.

Baer, D., Wolf, M., & Risley, R. (1968). Some current dimensions of applied behavior analysis. *Journal of Applied Behavior Analysis, 1*, 91–97.

Barlow, D. H., and Hersen, M., (1973). Single-case experimental designs: uses in applied clinical research. *Archives of General Psychiatry.* 29(3): 319–325.

Barlow, D. H. & Hersen, M. (1976). *Single case experimental designs: Strategies for studying behavior change.* New York: Pergamon.

Barlow, D. H. & Hersen, M. (1984). *Single case experimental designs: Strategies for studying behavior change* (2nd ed.). New York: Pergamon.

Bartlett, M. S. (1949). Fitting a straight line when both variables are subject to error, *Biometrics, 5,* 207–212.

Bergin, A. E. & Strupp, H. H. (1970). New directions in psychotherapy research: A summary statement. *Journal of Abnormal Psychology, 76,* 13–26.

Bijou, S. W. & Baer, D. M. (1961). *Child development: a systematic and empirical theory.* (Vol. 1). New York: Appleton-Century-Crofts.

Bloom, B. S. (1956). *Taxonomy of educational objectives, handbook I: the cognitive domain.* New York: David McKay Co., Inc.

Bolger, H. (1965). The case study method. In B. B. Wolman (Ed.), *Handbook of clinical psychology* (pp. 28–39). New York: McGraw-Hill.

Brown, G. W. & Mood, A. M. (1951). On median tests for linear hypotheses. In *Proceedings of the Second Berkeley Symposium on Mathematical Statistics and Probability.* Berkeley, CA: University of California Press.

Browne, R. H. (1979). On visual assessment of the significance of a mean difference. *Biometrics, 35,* 657–665.

Busk, P. L. & Marascuilo, L. A. (1988). Autocorrelation in single-subject research: a counter-argument to the myth of no autocorrelation. *Behavioral Assessment, 10,* 229–242.

Christ, T. J., & Coolong-Chaffin, M. (2007). Interpretations of curriculum-based measurement outcomes: Standard error and confidence intervals. *School Psychology Forum, 1,* 75–86.

Cliff, N. (1993). Dominance statistics: ordinal analyses to answer ordinal questions. *Psychological Bulletin, 114,* 494–509.

Cohen, J. (1960). A coefficient of agreement for nominal scales. *Educational and Psychological Measurement, 20,* 37–46.

Cooper, J. O., Heron, T. E., & Heward, W. L. (1987). *Applied behavior analysis.* Columbus, OH: Merrill.

Cottrell, A. & Lucchetti, R. (2009). *GNU Regression, Econometric and Time-series Library* [Computer Software]. Available at: http://gretl.sourceforge.net/.

Cramer, H. (1980). *Mathematical methods of statistics.* Princeton, NJ: Princeton University Press.

Crocker, L. & Algina, J. (2006). *Introduction to classical and modern test theory.* Pacific Grove, CA: Wadsworth.

Crocker, L. & Algina, J. (2008). *Introduction to classical and modern test theory.* New York: Holt, Rinehart and Winston.

D'Agostino, R. B., Campbell, M., & Greenhouse, J. (2006). Non-inferiority trials: continued advancements in concepts and methodology. *Statistics in Medicine, 25(7),* 1097–1099.

Delaney, H. D. & Vargha, A. (2002). Comparing several robust tests of stochastic equality with ordinally scaled variables and small to moderate sized samples. *Psychological Methods, 7,* 485–503.

DeProspero, A., & Cohen, S. (1979). Inconsistent visual analyses of intrasubject data. *Journal of Applied Behavior Analysis, 12 (4),* 573–579.

Djulbegovic B., Hozo I., Schwartz A., McMasters K. (1999). Acceptable regret in medical decision making. *Medical Hypotheses, 53,* 253–259.

Draper, N. R. & Smith, H. (1998). *Applied regression analysis* (3rd ed.). New York, NY: John Wiley & Sons.

Dukes, W. F. (1965). N = 1. *Psychological Bulletin, 64,* 74–79.

Emerson, J. D. & Hoaglin, D. C. (1983). Resistant lines for y-versus-x. In D. C. Hoaglin, F. Mosteller & J. W. Tukey (Eds.), *Understanding robust and exploratory data analysis* (pp. 129–165), New York: John Wiley & Sons.

Estes, W. K. (1956). The problem of inference from curves based on group data. *Psychological Bulletin,* 53, 134–140.

Fisher, R. A. (1915). Frequency distribution of the values of the correlation coefficient in samples from an indefinitely large population. *Biometrika, 10 (4),* 507–521.

Fleiss, J. L. & Cohen, J. (1973). The equivalence of weighted kappa and the intraclass correlation coefficient as measures of reliability. *Educational and Psychological Measurement, 33,* 613–619.

Franklin, R. D., Allison, D. B., & Gorman, B. S. (1997). *Design and analysis of single-case research.* New Jersey: Lawrence Erlbaum Associates.

Franklin, R. D., Gorman, B. S., Beasley, M. T., & Allison, D. B. (1997). Graphical display and visual analysis. Chapter 5. In Franklin, R. D., Allison, D. B., & Gorman, B. S. (Eds.), *Design and Analysis of Single-Case Research* (pp. 119–158). Hillsdale, NJ: Lawrence Erlbaum Associates.

Furlong, M. J. & Wampold, B. E. (1982). Intervention effects and relative variation as dimensions in experts' use of visual inspection. *Journal of Applied Behavioral Analysis, 15,* 415–421.

Ghiselli, E. E. Campbell, J. P., & Zedeck, S. (1981). *Measurement theory for the behavioral sciences.* San Francisco, CA: W. H. Freeman & Co.

Gibson, G. & Ottenbacher, K. (1988). Characteristics influencing the visual analysis of single-subject data: An empirical analysis. *Journal of Applied Behavioral Science, 24(3),* 298–314.

Gibson, W. M. & Jowett, G. H. (1957). Three-group regression analysis, part I. Simple regression analysis. *Applied Statistics, 6,* 114–122.

Goldstein H. & Healy M. J. R. (1995). The graphical presentation of a collection of means. *Journal of the Royal Statistical Society A, 158(1),* 175–177.

Goodman, L. A. & Kruskal, W. H. (1954). Measures of association for cross classification I. *Journal of the American Statistical Association, 49,* 732–764.

Goodman, L. A. & Kruskal, W. H. (1959). Measures of association for cross classification II: Further discussion and references. *Journal of the American Statistical Association, 52,* 123–163.

Goodman, L. A. & Kruskal, W. H. (1963). Measures of association for cross classification III: Approximate Sampling Theory. *Journal of the American Statistical Association, 58,* 310–364.

Granato, G. E., (2006). *Kendall-Theil Robust Line (KTRLine), Version 1.0* [Computer Software]. Available at: http://pubs.usgs.gov/tm/2006/tm4a7/.

Graybill, F. A. & Iyer, H. K. (1998). *Regression Analysis: Concepts and Applications.* Belmont, CA: Duxbury Press.

Greenspan, P. & Fisch, G. S. (1992). *Visual inspection of data: a statistical analysis of behavior.* Proceedings of the Annual Meeting of the American Statistical Association, Alexandria, VA.

Greenwald, A. G. (1976). Within-subjects designs: to use or not to use? *Psychological Bulletin, 8,* 314–320.

Grissom, R. J. & Kim, J. J. (2005). *Effect sizes for research: a broad practical approach.* Mahwah, NJ: Lawrence Erlbaum Associates, Inc.

Guilford, J. P. (1954). *Psychometric methods.* New York: McGraw-Hill.

Harbst, K. B., Ottenbacher, K. J., & Harris, S. R. (1991). Interrater reliability of therapists' judgments of graphed data. *Physical Therapy, 71,* 107–115.

Hedges, L. V. & Olkin, I. (1985). *Statistical methods for meta-analysis.* Academic Press: San Diego, CA.

Helsel, D. R. & Hirsch, R. M. (1992). *Statistical methods in water resources.* New York, NY: Elsevier.

Helsel, D. R. & Hirsch, R. M. (2002). Statistical methods in water resources. *Techniques of Water-Resources Investigations.* Available at: http://water.usgs.gov/pubs/twri/twri4a3/.

Hersen, M. & Barlow, D. H. (eds.) (1976). *Single case experimental designs: strategies for studying behavior change.* Oxford, UK: Pergamon.

Hintze, J. (2006). *NCSS and PASS: Number Cruncher Statistical Systems,* [Computer software]. Kaysville, UT. Available at: www.ncss.com.

Hirsch, R. M. & Slack, J. R. (1984). A nonparametric trend test for seasonal data with serial dependence. *Water Resources Research, 20(6),* 727–732.

Hoaglin, D. C., Mosteller, F., & Tukey, J. W. (1983). *Understanding robust and exploratory data analysis.* New York, NY: John Wiley & Sons.

Hofmann, D. (2005) Common sources of errors in measurement systems. In P. H. Sydenham & R. Thorn (eds.), *The handbook of measuring systems design* (pp. 289–294). New York, NY: John Wiley & Sons.

Hojem, M. A. & Ottenbacher, K. J. (1988). Empirical investigation of visual-inspection versus trend-line analysis of single-subject data. *Journal of the American Physical Therapy Association, 68,* 983–988.

Hollander, M. & Wolfe, D. A. (1999). *Nonparametric statistical methods* (2nd ed.). New York, NY: John Wiley & Sons.

Horner, R., & Spaulding, S. (2010). Single-case research designs. In N. J. Salkind (Ed.), *Encyclopedia of research design* (pp. 1386–1394). Thousand Oaks, CA: Sage Publications.

Horner, R. H., Albin, R. A., Todd, A. W., Newton, S. J., & Sprague, J. R. (2010). Designing and implementing individualized positive behavior support. In M.E. Snell & F. Brown (Eds.), *Instruction of Students with Severe Disabilities* (pp. 225–257). Upper Saddle River, NJ: Pearson Education.

Huitema, B. E. (1986). Autocorrelation in behavioral research: wherefore art thou? In A. Poling & R. W. Fuqua (eds.), *Research methods in applied behavior analysis: issues and advances* (pp. 187–208) New York: Plenum.

Ioannidis, J. P. (2005). Why most published research findings are false. *PLOS Medicine, 2(8),* e124. doi:10.1371/journal.pmed.0020124.

Johnson, I. & Velleman, P. F. (1985). Efficient scores, variance decompositions, and Monte Carlo swindles. *Journal of the American Statistical Association, 80*, 851–862.

Jones, R. R., Weinrott, M., & Vaught, R. S. (1978). Time-series analysis in operant research. *Journal of Applied Behavior Analysis, 10*, 151–166.

Kazdin, A. E. (1982). *Single-case research designs: methods for clinical and applied settings.* New York: Oxford University Press.

Kazdin, A. E. (2010). *Single-case research designs: methods for clinical and applied settings* (2nd ed.). New York: Oxford University Press.

Kendall, M. G. (1938). A new measure of rank correlation. *Biometrika, 30 (1)*, 81–93.

Kennedy, C. H. (2005). *Single-case designs for educational research.* Boston: Allyn and Bacon.

Keppel, G. (1982). *Design and analysis: a researcher's handbook* (2nd ed.). Englewood Cliffs, NJ: Prentice-Hall.

Knapp, T. J. (1983). Behavior analysts' visual appraisal of behavior change in graphic display. *Behavioral Assessment, 5*, 155–164.

Koenig, C. (1972). *Charting the future course of behavior.* Kansas City, KS: Precision Media.

Kratochwill, T. R. (ed.). (1978). *Single subject research: strategies for evaluating change.* New York: Academic Press.

Kratochwill, T. R. & Levin, J. R. (eds.) (1992). *Single-case research design and analysis: new directions for psychology and education.* Hillsdale, NJ: Lawrence Erlbaum Associates.

Kratochwill, T. R., Hitchcock, J., Horner, R. H., Levin, J. R., Odom, S. L., Rindskopf, D. M., & Shadish, W. R. (2010). *Single-case designs technical documentation.* Available at: http://ies.ed.gov/ncee/wwc/pdf/wwc_scd.pdf.

Leitenberg, H. (1973). The use of single-case methodology in psychotherapy research. *Journal of Abnormal Psychology, 82(1)*, 87–101.

Lowry, R. (2010). *Kappa as a Measure of Concordance in Categorical Sorting.* [Web-Based Software]. Available at: http://faculty.vassar.edu/lowry/kappa.html.

Ma, H. H. (2006). An alternative method for quantitative synthesis of single-subject research: percentage of data points exceeding the median. *Behavior Modification, 30*, 598–617.

Manolov, R. & Solanas, A. (2008). Comparing N=1 effect size indices in presence of autocorrelation. *Behavior Modification, 32(6)*, 860–875.

Matyas, T. A. & Greenwood, K. M. (1990). Visual analysis of single-case time series: effects of variability, serial dependence, and magnitude of intervention effects. *Journal of Applied Behavior Analysis, 23*, 341–351.

Matyas, T. A. & Greenwood, K. M. (1996). Serial dependency in single-case time series. In R. D. Franklin, D. B. Allison, & B. S. Gorman (eds.), *Design and Analysis of Single-Case Research* (pp. 215–243). Mahwah, NJ: Lawrence Erlbaum Associates.

McBride, G. (2000). Anomalies and remedies in nonparametric seasonal Kendall trend tests and estimates. NIWA (Hamilton, NZ), from the National Institute of Water and Atmospheric Research, Ltd. (New Zealand) Improved Statistical Methods page. Available at: www.niwa.co.nz.

McCabe, G. P. (1980). Use of the 27% rule in experimental design. *Communications in Statistics, Part A: Theory and Methods, 9,* 765–776.

Michael, J. L. (1974). Statistical inference for individual organism research: mixed blessing or curse? *Journal of Applied Behavior Analysis, 7,* 647–653.

Miller, B. (2010). *OPENSTAT.* [Software]. Available at: www.statpages.org/miller/openstat/.

Mosteller, F. (1946). On some useful "inefficient" statistics. *Annals of Mathematical Statistics, 17 (4),* 377–408.

Nair, K. R. & Shrivastava, M. P. (1942). On a simple method of curve fitting. *Sankhaya, 6,* 121–132.

Neter, J., Kutner, M. H., Nachtsheim, C. J., & Wasserman, W. (1996). *Applied linear statistical models* (4th ed.). Boston, MA: McGraw-Hill.

Nourbakhsh, M. R. & Ottenbacher, K. J. (1994). The statistical analysis of single-subject data: a comparative examination. *Physical Therapy, 74,* 80–88.

Ottenbacher, K. J. (1986). An analysis of serial dependency in occupational therapy research. *Occupational Therapy Journal of Research, 6,* 211–216.

Ottenbacher, K. J. (1990). Visual inspection of single-subject data: an empirical analysis. *Mental Retardation, 28,* 283–290.

Park, H., Marascuilo, L., & Gaylord-Ross, R. (1990). Visual inspection and statistical analysis of single-case designs. *Journal of Experimental Education, 58,* 311–320.

Parker, R. I. (2006). Increased reliability for single case research results: is the bootstrap the answer? *Behavior Therapy, 37(4),* 326–338.

Parker, R. I. & Vannest, K. J. (2009). An improved effect size for single-case research: Nonoverlap of all pairs. *Behavior Therapy, 40,* 357–367.

Parker, R. I., Cryer, J., & Byrns, G. (2006). Controlling trend in single case research. *School Psychology Quarterly, 21(3),* 418–440.

Parker, R. I., Vannest, K. J., & Brown, L. (2009). The improvement rate difference for single case research. *Exceptional Children, 75(2),* 135–150.

Parker, R. I., Vannest, K. J., & Davis, J. L. (2011). Effect size in single case research: a review of nine non-overlap techniques. *Behavior Modification,* DOI: 10.1177/0145445511399147.

Parker, R. I., Vannest, K. J., & Davis, J. L. (2012). A simple method to control positive baseline trend within data non overlap. *Journal of Special Education.* Published online, 22 August. Available at: http://journalofspecialeducation.sagepub.com. DOI 10.1177/0022466912456430.

Parker, R. I., Vannest, K. J., & Davis, J. L. (in press). Reliability for multi-category rating scales. *Journal of School Psychology.*

Parker, R. I., Vannest, K. J., Davis, J. L., & Clemens, N. H. (2012). Defensible progress monitoring data for medium/high-stakes decisions. *Journal of Special Education, 46 (3),* 141–151.

Parker, R. I., Vannest, K. J., Davis, J. L., & Sauber, S. B. (2011). Combining non-overlap and trend for single case research: Tau-U. *Behavior Therapy, 42,* 284–299.

Parsonson, B. S. & Baer, D. M. (1978). The analysis and presentation of graphic data. In T. R. Kratochwill (ed.), *Single-subject research. Strategies for evaluating change* (pp. 101–165). New York: Academic Press.

Parsonson, B. S. & Baer, D. M. (1986). The graphic analysis of data. In A. Poling & R. W. Fuqua (eds.), *Research methods in applied behavior analysis: issues and advances* (pp. 157–186). New York: Plenum.

Parsonson, B. S. & Baer, D. M. (1992). The visual analysis of data, and current research into the stimuli controlling it. In T. R. Kratochwill & J. R. Levin (eds.), *Single-case research design and analysis* (pp. 15–40). Hillsdale, NJ: Lawrence Erlbaum Associates.

Paul, G. L. (1969). Behavior modification research: design and tactics. In C. M. Franks (ed.), *Behavior therapy: appraisal and status* (pp. 29–62). New York: McGraw-Hill.

Pawlicki, R. (1970). Behaviour-therapy research with children: a critical review. *Canadian Journal of Behavioural Science 2(3),* 163–173.

Payton, M. E., Greenstone, M. H., & Schenker, N. (2003). Overlapping confidence intervals or standard error intervals: what do they mean in terms of statistical significance? *Journal of Insect Science,* 3(34), 1–6.

Payton, M. E., Miller, A. E., & Raun, W. R. (2000). Testing statistical hypotheses using standard error bars and confidence intervals. *Communications in Soil Science and Plant Analysis.* 31, 547–552.

Preston, D., & Carter, M. (2009). A review of the efficacy of the picture exchange communication system intervention. *Journal of Autism and Developmental Disorders, 39,* 1471–1486.

Reynolds, C. R., Livingston, R. B., Willson, V. L. (2006). *Measurement and assessment in education.* Boston: Allyn and Bacon.

Rojahn, J. & Schulze, H.-H. (1985). The linear regression line as a judgmental aid in the visual analysis of serially dependent A–B time-series data. *Journal of Psychopathology and Behavioral Assessment, 7,* 191–206.

Roos, C. F. (1937). Some geometrical considerations in the general theory of fitting lines and planes, *Metron, 13(1),* 3–20.

Rush, A. J., First, M. B., & Blacker, D. (2008). *Handbook of psychiatric measures* (2nd ed.). Washington, DC: American Psychiatric Publishing, Inc.

Rutherford, R. B., Quinn, M. M., & Mathur, S. R. (eds.) (2004). *Handbook of research in emotional behavioral disorders.* New York: Guilford.

Salkind, N. J. (ed.) (2007). *The encyclopedia of measurement and statistics, (Vol. 1).* Thousand Oaks, CA: Sage.

Schenker, N. & Gentleman, J. F. (2001). On judging the significance of differences by examining overlap between confidence intervals. *The American Statistician, 55,* 182–186.

Schwarz, C. J. (2007). *Sampling, regression, experimental design and analysis for environmental scientists, biologists and resource managers.* British Columbia, Canada: Simon Fraser University. Available at: www.stat.sfu.ca/~cschwarz/Stat-650/Notes/PDF/Chapter17.pdf.

Scruggs, T. E. & Mastropieri, M. A. (1994). The utility of the PND statistic: a reply to Allison and Gorman. *Behavior, Research, and Therapy, 32*, 879–883.

Scruggs, T. E. & Mastropieri, M. A. (1998). Summarizing single-subject research: issues and applications. *Behavior Modification, 22*, 221–242.

Scruggs, T.E., & Mastropieri, M.A. (2001). How to summarize single-participant research: ideas and applications. *Exceptionality 9*, 227–244.

Scruggs, T. E., Mastropieri, M. A., & Casto, G. (1987). The quantitative synthesis of single subject research: methodology and validation. *Remedial and Special Education, 8(2)*, 24–33.

Sen, P. K. (1968). Estimates of the regression coefficient based on Kendall's tau. *American Statistical Association Journal, 63*, 1379–1389.

Shadish, W. R. & Haddock, C. K. (1994). Combining estimates of effect size. In H. M. Cooper & L. V. Hedges (eds.), *The handbook of research synthesis* (pp. 261–281). New York: Russell Sage Foundation.

Shadish, W. R., Cook, T. D., & Campbell, D. T. (2002). *Experimental and quasi-experimental designs for generalized causal inference*. Boston, MA: Houghton Mifflin.

Shapiro, M. B. (1961). The single case in fundamental clinical psychological research. *British Journal of Medical Psychology, 35*, 255–262.

Sheskin, D. J. (2007). *Handbook of parametric and nonparametric statistical procedures*, (4th ed.). Boca Raton, FL: Chapman and Hall.

Sidman, M. (1960). *Tactics for scientific research: evaluating experimental data in psychology*. New York: Basic Books.

Siegel, S. & Castellan, N. J., Jr. (1988). *Nonparametric statistics for the behavioral sciences* (2nd ed.). New York, NY: McGraw–Hill.

Simkins, L. D. (1969). *The basis of psychology as a behavioural science*. Waltham, MA: Blaisdell Publishing Company.

Skiba, R., Deno, S. L., Marston, D. E., & Casey, A. (1989). Influence of trend estimate and subject familiarity on practitioners' judgements of intervention effectiveness. *Journal of Special Education, 22(4)*, 433–446.

Skinner, B. F. (1966). The phylogeny and ontogeny of behavior. *Science, 153*, 1205–1213.

Smith, A. (1863). *An inquiry into the nature and causes of the wealth of nations*. Edinburgh, Scotland: Adam and Charles Black.

Smith, S. L., Vannest, K. J., & Davis, J. L. (2011). Seven reliability indices for high-stakes decision making: description, selection, and simple calculation. *Psychology in the Schools, 48(10)*, 1064–1075. DOI: 10.1002/pits.20610

Stats Direct (2008). *Stats Direct Statistical Software* [Computer software]. London: Stats Direct. Retrieved from www.statsdirect.com.

Stigler, S. M. (1974). Linear functions of order statistics with smooth weight functions. *Annals of Statistics. 2(4)*, 676–93.

Suen, H. K. & Lee, P. S. C. (1985). Effects of the use of percentage agreement on behavioral observation reliabilities: a reassessment. *Journal of Psychopathology and Behavioral Assessment, 7(3)*, 221–234.

SYSTAT (2008). *Mystat Software, Version 11* [Computer Software]. Available at: www.systat.com.

Tawney, J. W. & Gast, D. L. (1984). *Single subject research in special education.* Columbus, OH: Merrill.

Theil, H. (1950). A rank-invariant method of linear and polynomial regression analysis, I, II, III. *Proceedings of the Koninklijke Nederlandse Akademie van Wetenschappen A, 53,* 386–392, 521–535, 1397–1412.

Tukey, J. W. (1977). *Exploratory data analysis.* Menlo Park, CA: Addison-Wesley.

Vannest, K. J., Reynolds, C., & Kamphaus, R. (2008). *BASC-2 intervention guide for learning and behavior problems.* Minneapolis, MN: Pearson.

Vannest, K. J. Parker, R. I., Davis, J. L., Soares, D. A., & Smith, S. L. (2012) The Theil-Sen slope for high stakes decisions from progress monitoring. *Behavioral Disorders 37 (4).*

Vannest, K. J., Davis, J. L., Davis, C. R., Mason, B. A., & Burke, M. D. (2010). Effective intervention with a daily behavior report card: A meta-analysis. *School Psychology Review, 39,* 654–672.

Von Storch, H. (1995). Misuses of statistical analysis in climate research. In H.V. Storch & A. Navarra (Eds.). *Analysis of climate variability: applications of statistical techniques* (pp.11–26). New York: Springer-Verlag.

Wainer, H. (1990). *Picturing the uncertain world: how to understand, communicate and control uncertainty through graphical display.* Princeton, NJ: Princeton University Press.

Wald, A. (1940). The fitting of straight lines if both variables are subject to error. *Annals of Mathematical Statistics, 11,* 284–300.

Wampold, B. E. & Furlong, M. J. (1981). Randomizations test in single-subject designs: illustrative examples. *Journal of Psychopathology and Behavioral Assessment, 3(4),* 329–341.

White, O. R. (1987). Some comments concerning: The quantitative synthesis of single-subject research. *Remedial and Special Education, 8 (2),* 34–39.

White, O. R. & Haring, N. G. (1980). *Exceptional teaching: a multimedia training package.* Columbus, OH: Merrill.

White, O. R., Rusch, F. R., Kazdin, A. E., & Hartmann, D. P. (1989). Applications of meta analysis in individual subject research. *Behavioral Assessment, 11,* 281–296.

Wilcox, R. R. (1998). Simulations on the Theil-Sen regression estimator with right-censored data. *Statistics and Probability Letters, 39,* 43–47.

Wilcox, R. R. (2010). *Fundamentals of modern statistical methods: substantially improving power and accuracy* (2nd ed.). New York, NY: Springer.

Wolery, M., Busick, M., Reichow, B., & Barton, E. (2010). Comparison of overlap methods for quantitatively synthesizing single-subject data. *Journal of Special Education, 44(1),* 18–28.

INDEX

Taylor & Francis

eBooks
FOR LIBRARIES

ORDER YOUR
FREE 30 DAY
INSTITUTIONAL
TRIAL TODAY!

Over 23,000 eBook titles in the Humanities,
Social Sciences, STM and Law from some of the
world's leading imprints.

Choose from a range of subject packages or create your own!

Benefits for
you

▶ Free MARC records
▶ COUNTER-compliant usage statistics
▶ Flexible purchase and pricing options

Benefits
for your
user

▶ Off-site, anytime access via Athens or referring URL
▶ Print or copy pages or chapters
▶ Full content search
▶ Bookmark, highlight and annotate text
▶ Access to thousands of pages of quality research
  at the click of a button

For more information, pricing enquiries or to order
a free trial, contact your local online sales team.

UK and Rest of World: **online.sales@tandf.co.uk**

US, Canada and Latin America:
e-reference@taylorandfrancis.com

www.ebooksubscriptions.com

ALPSP Award for
BEST eBOOK
PUBLISHER
2009 Finalist
sponsored by

Taylor & Francis eBooks
Taylor & Francis Group

A flexible and dynamic resource for teaching, learning and research.